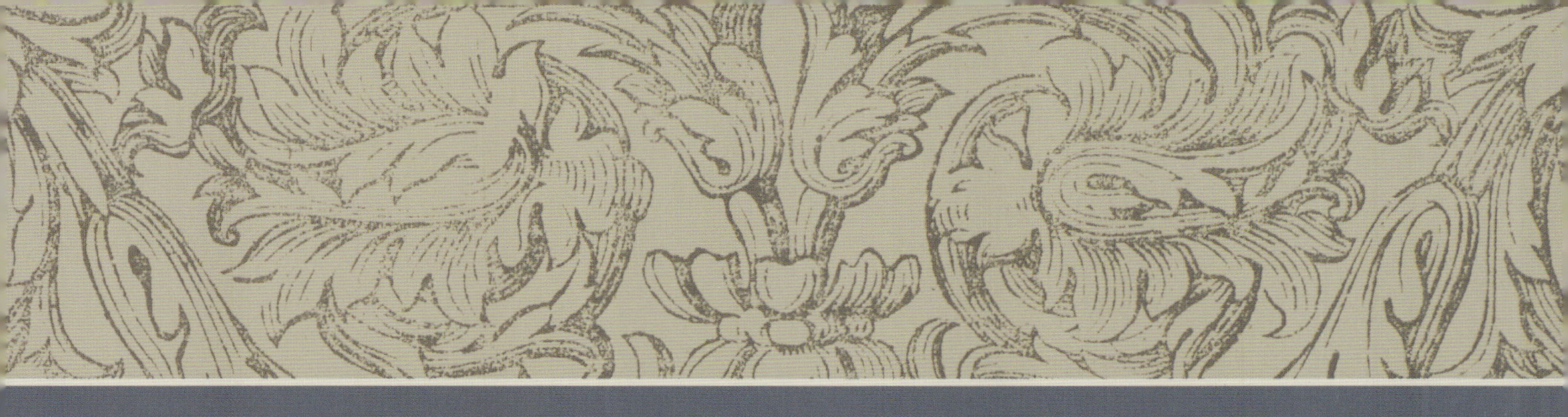

Introducing
Italian Art

Glasgow Museums

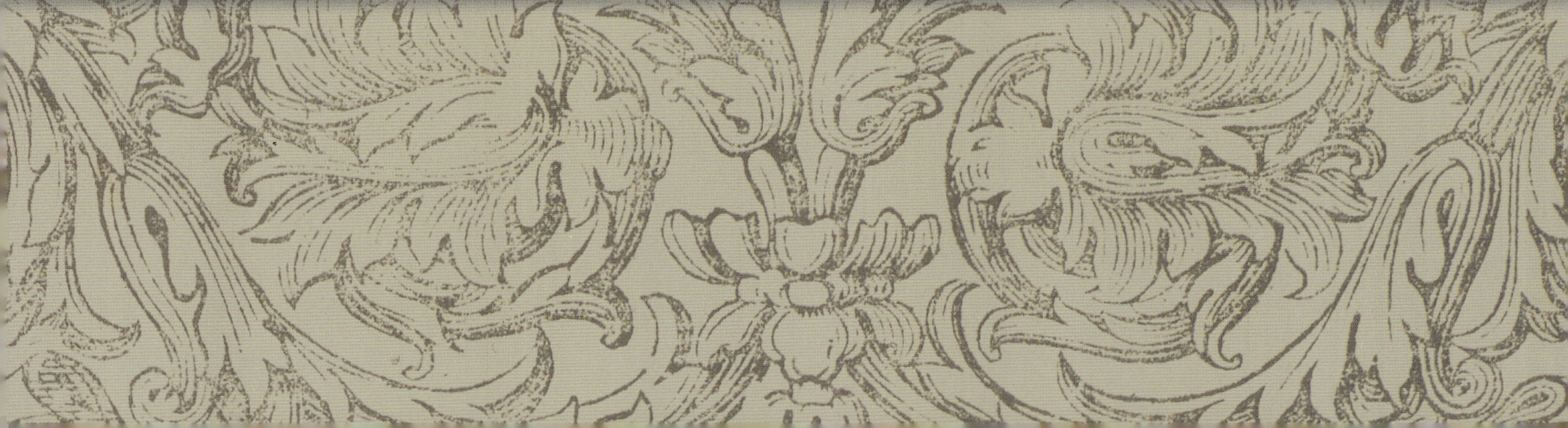

Published to accompany the exhibitions
The Essence of Beauty: 500 Years of Italian Art
Kelvingrove Art Gallery and Museum
6 April–12 August 2012
&
The Splendour of Italian Art 1400–1900
Compton Verney, Warwickshire
23 March–23 June 2013

First published in 2012 by Culture and Sport Glasgow
(Glasgow Museums)

ISBN 978-1-908638-00-7

www.glasgowmuseums.com

Front cover image:
St Catherine Crowned,
*c.*1520, Bartolomeo
Veneto

Author: Patricia Collins
Edited by: Fiona MacLeod
Designed by: Fiona MacDonald
Photography: Maureen Kinnear
Picture research: Winnie Tyrrell
Digital imaging: Alan Broadfoot
Printed in Scotland by Allander

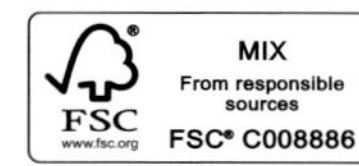

Acknowledgements

All efforts have been made to trace copyright holders but
if any have been inadvertently omitted please notify the
publishers.

CONTENTS

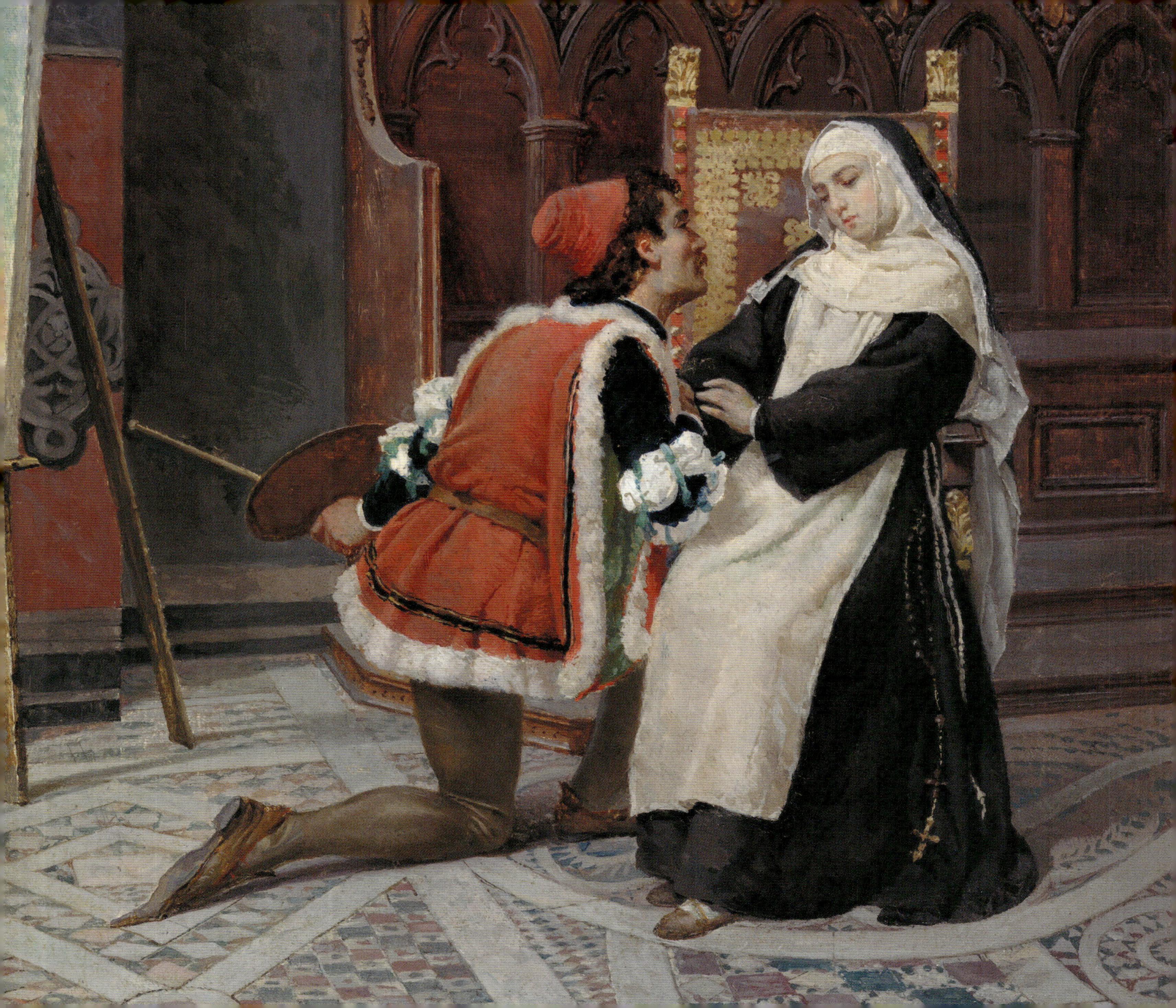

Glasgow's Italian Paintings

There are around 150 Italian paintings in Glasgow Museums' collection. Many of the finest works are featured here, where they are complemented by other high-quality Italian artefacts. Together they represent five centuries' worth of raw talent tempered by craftsmanship of an exceptional standard.

The earliest painting dates from the last quarter of the fourteenth century; the latest was painted towards the end of the nineteenth century. All have their own individually-defined character. Some are by very famous artists, others by lesser-known (or even anonymous) makers; many are religious works, meant to be used as a focus for prayer and meditation. Others are linked to literature, and some just express pure joy in the world around.

Although the two paintings illustrated here bookend the entire period covered in this selection of paintings, there is an unexpected link between them. The earliest work in the collection, *St Lawrence*, once part of a late medieval altarpiece, was painted by the Sienese artist Niccolò di Buonaccorso. The much later painting, dating from about 1879, is by Pietro Aldi, who also trained in Siena. It harks back to the late medieval style, and the setting is a room which still exists in Siena's Palazzo Pubblico. There is a fresco on the wall which was painted around 1407–8, just 10 years or so after Niccolò's death.

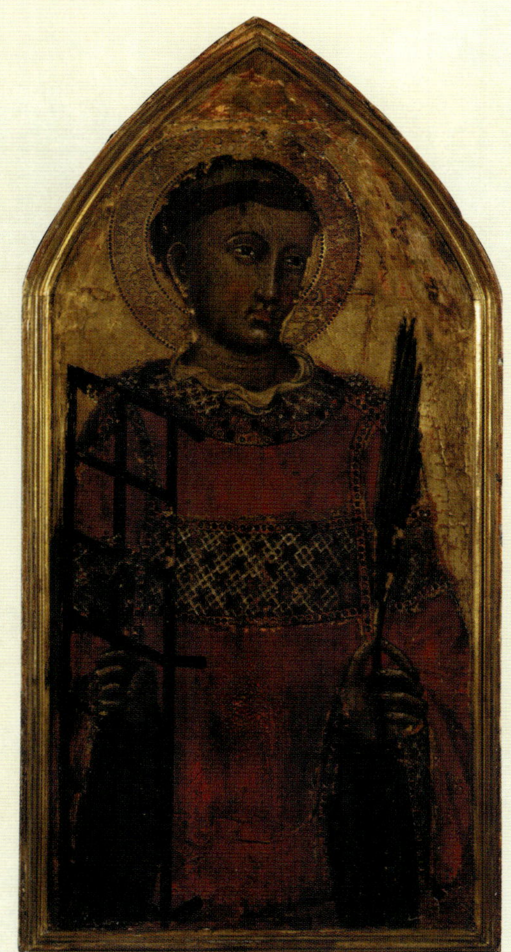

Archibald McLellan, 1906
Robert Cree Crawford
(after John Graham Gilbert)

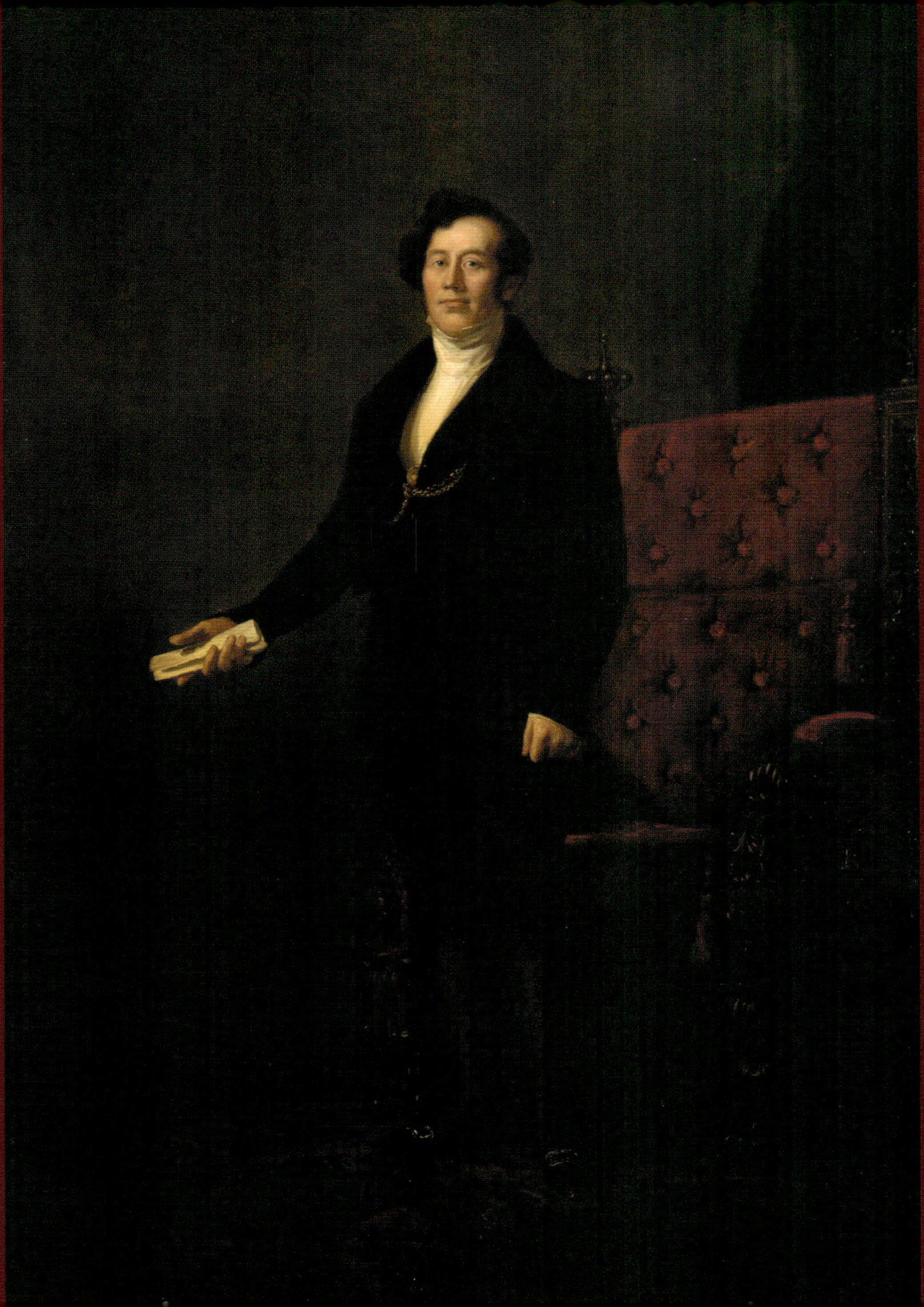

In 1854 the coach-builder Archibald McLellan (1797–1854) bequeathed his extensive art collection, including Italian paintings, to Glasgow. McLellan's desire was for the collection to be '…of some use to those who are desirous of studying the progress of art; … it may be made to form the foundation for a more extensive and complete collection…'.

As McLellan anticipated, paintings from other locally-based art collections were donated to the city, and the holdings of Italian paintings now numbers some 150 works. Among the most generous gifts were 12 fine Italian paintings bequeathed in 1877 by the widow of the portrait painter, collector and friend of McLellan, John Graham Gilbert (1794–1866).

Paintings from the collections of James Young (1811–83) and others also joined the city's collection, as did a pair of Neoclassical paintings by Vincenzo Camuccini, bequeathed by Cecilia Douglas (1772–1862), who had commissioned them in Rome during the 1820s.

Two collections which included world-class Italian works of art were given to the city in the twentieth century. In 1944, Sir William and Constance, Lady Burrell, presented their collection, and in 1967 Mrs Anne Maxwell Macdonald gave Pollok House, its surrounding parkland, and the Stirling Maxwell collection of paintings, founded by her grandfather, Sir William Stirling Maxwell (1818–78).

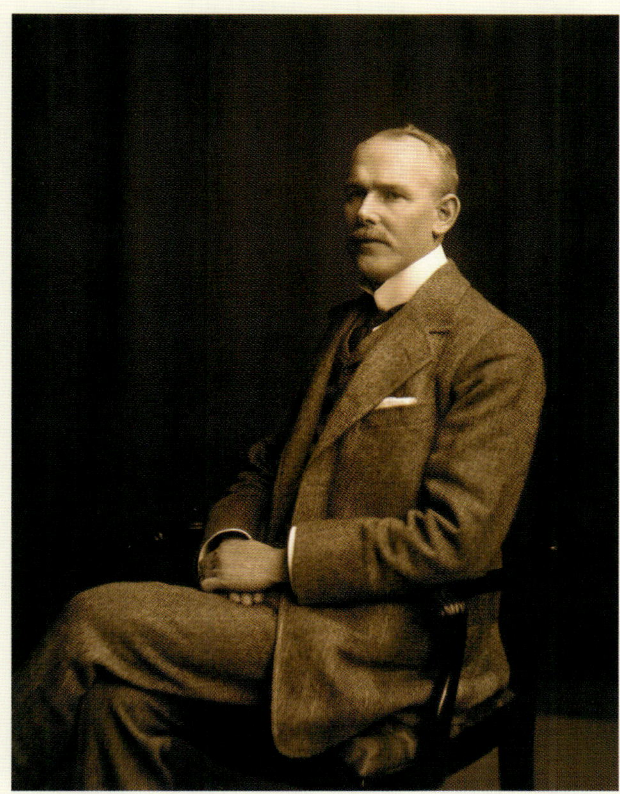

Sir William Burrell

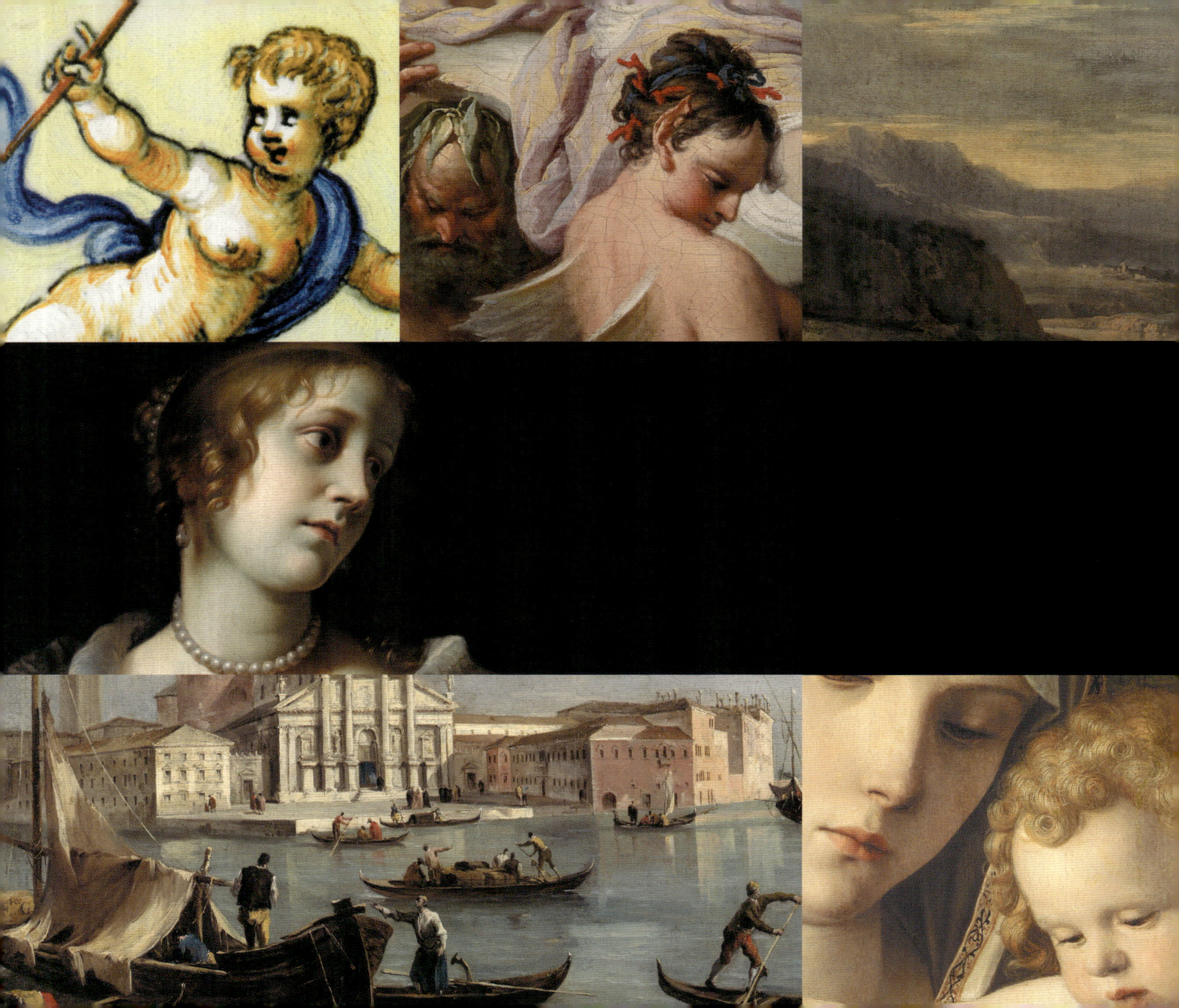

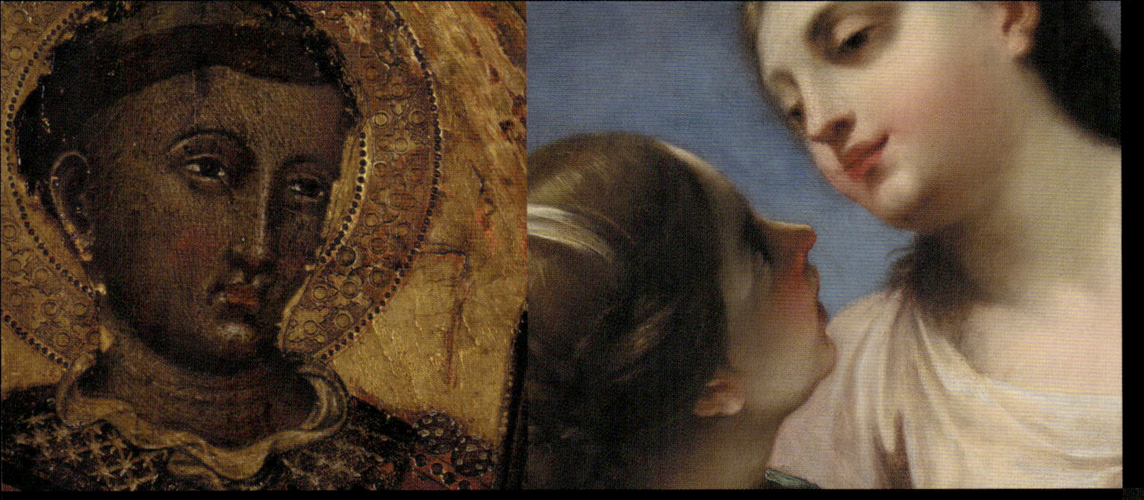

Introducing
Italian Art

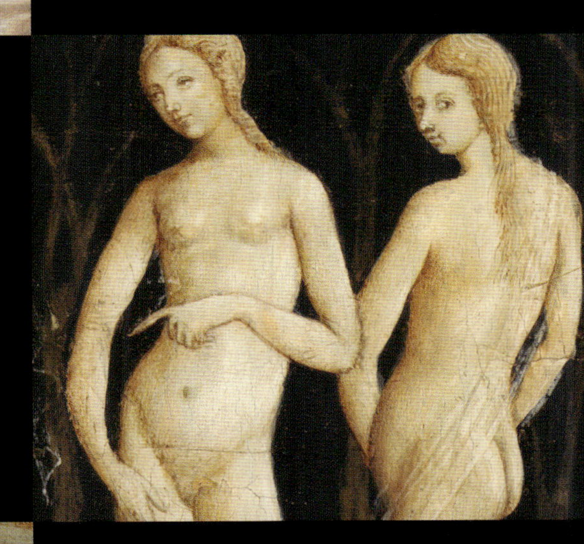

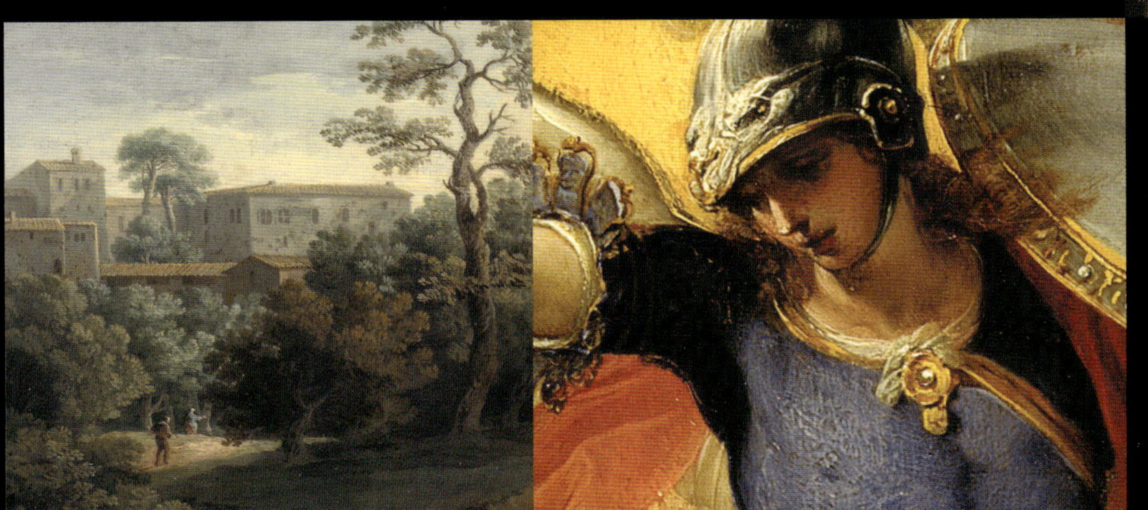

Against an uncertain background of violent conflict and infectious disease, the art of the fourteenth and fifteenth centuries was almost entirely religious in nature. The Roman Catholic Church was all-powerful. Men and women in religious orders ministered to the sick, and high-ranking churchmen utilized art and architecture as symbols of status and power.

Independent rulers of city-states, such as Florence and Siena, were continually in conflict, as were individual families within towns and cities, later described by Shakespeare in his play *Romeo and Juliet*. Dynastic alliances between families, towns, cities and even countries were strategically planned and often short-lived. Even popes retained – and many led – their own armies.

Simultaneously scholars were gradually widening the scope of their studies to include non-religious subjects. The writings of both Greek and Latin authors were studied. The development of the printing press was key to the spread of both images and ideas from the classical world. By 1500 Venice was a thriving centre of the printing industry, and artists and artisans took full advantage of this new source of material.

During the sixteenth century violence was still ever-present in Italy, never more so than during the Sack of Rome in 1527, when the holy city was overrun and looted by German troops on the orders of the Habsburg Emperor Charles V. Most men carried weapons as a matter of course; these were functional but were also seen as fashionable accessories.

Artists carried on working despite hostilities. Technical and stylistic changes in art which had begun in the previous century, like the development of mathematical perspective and the use of oil to bind coloured pigments, became normal practice. Inspiration derived from classical sources was now commonplace too; even commissions from religious patrons often featured subjects based on ancient literary sources.

In Germany, the anti-Roman Church uprising known as the Reformation was gradually gathering support. Protestant objections to religious art were to have major implications in Catholic and non-Catholic countries alike.

By the seventeenth century Italy still consisted of independent states, but many were dominated by Spanish interests, represented by the Habsburg ruling dynasty. In the years following the Protestant uprising, a period now known as the Counter Reformation, Spanish support for the Roman Catholic Church was crucial. It was during this time that the Holy Office of the Inquisition (known as the Spanish Inquisition), became most active in re-converting and punishing heretics – those who

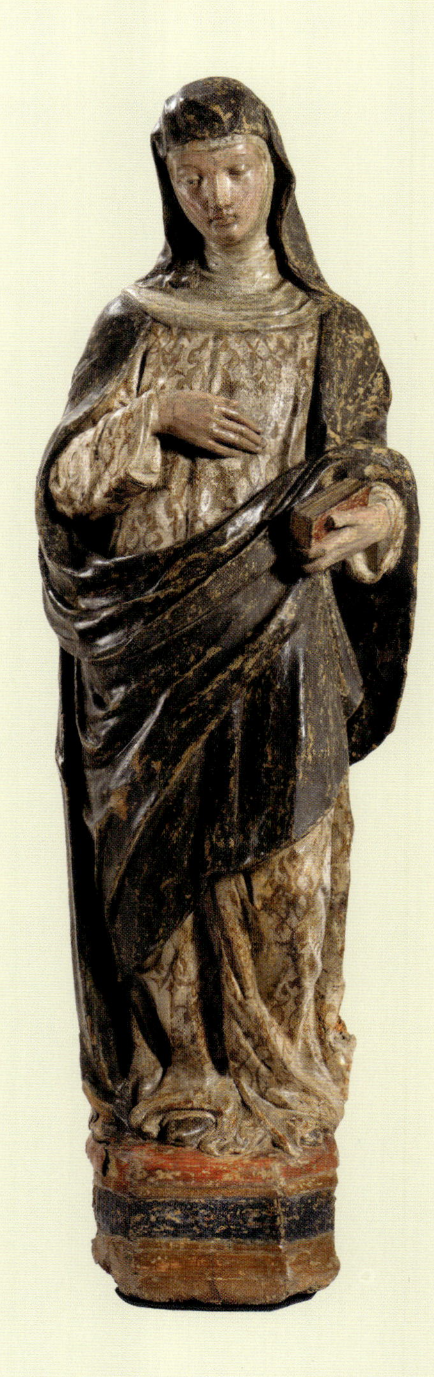

St Catherine of Siena, *c.*1480
Attributed to Neroccio de' Landi

Caterina Benincasa (1347–80), was patron saint of her home city, Siena. A Dominican sister, she was canonized in 1461. This sculpture might have been housed in a church or convent.

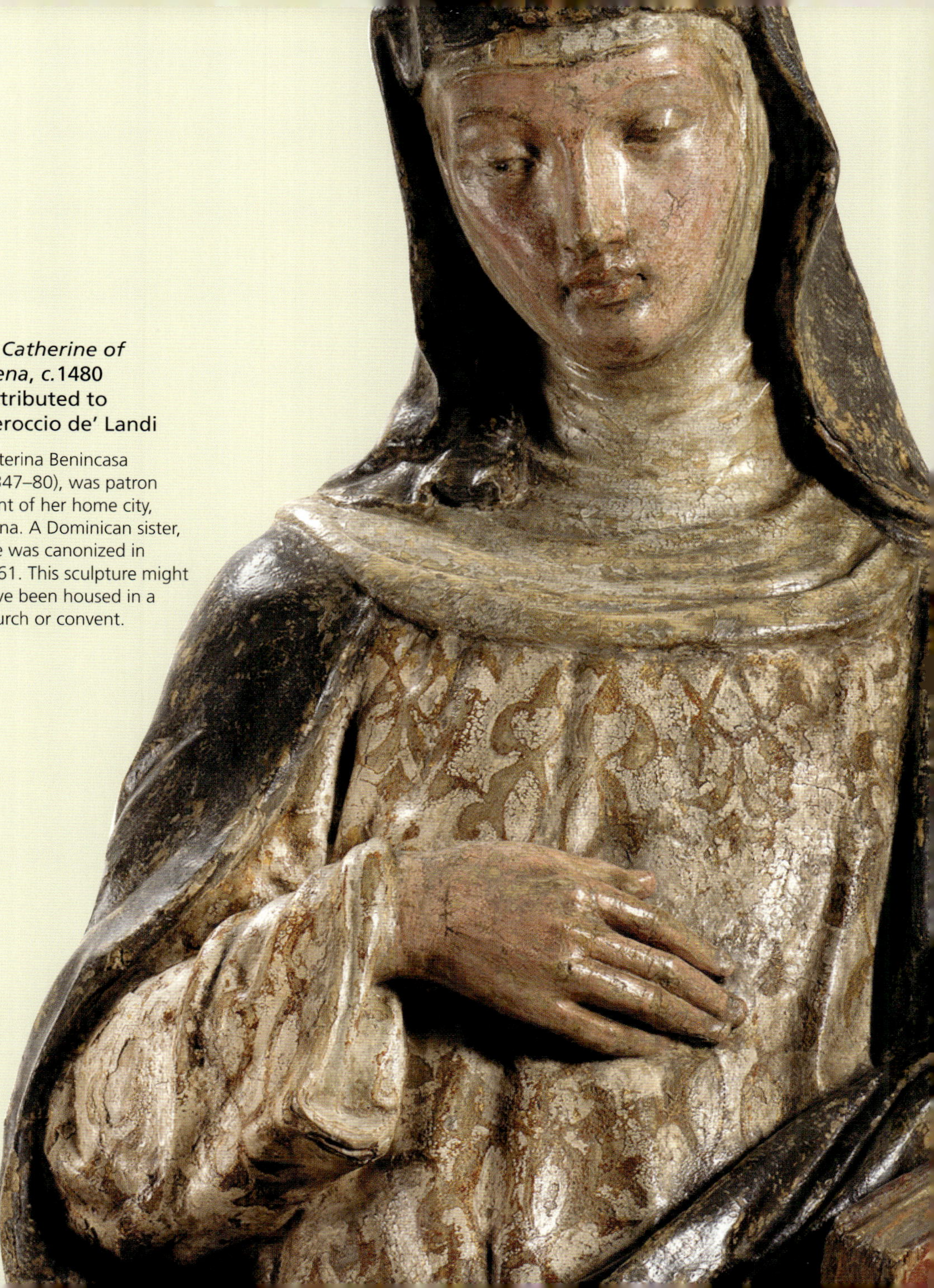

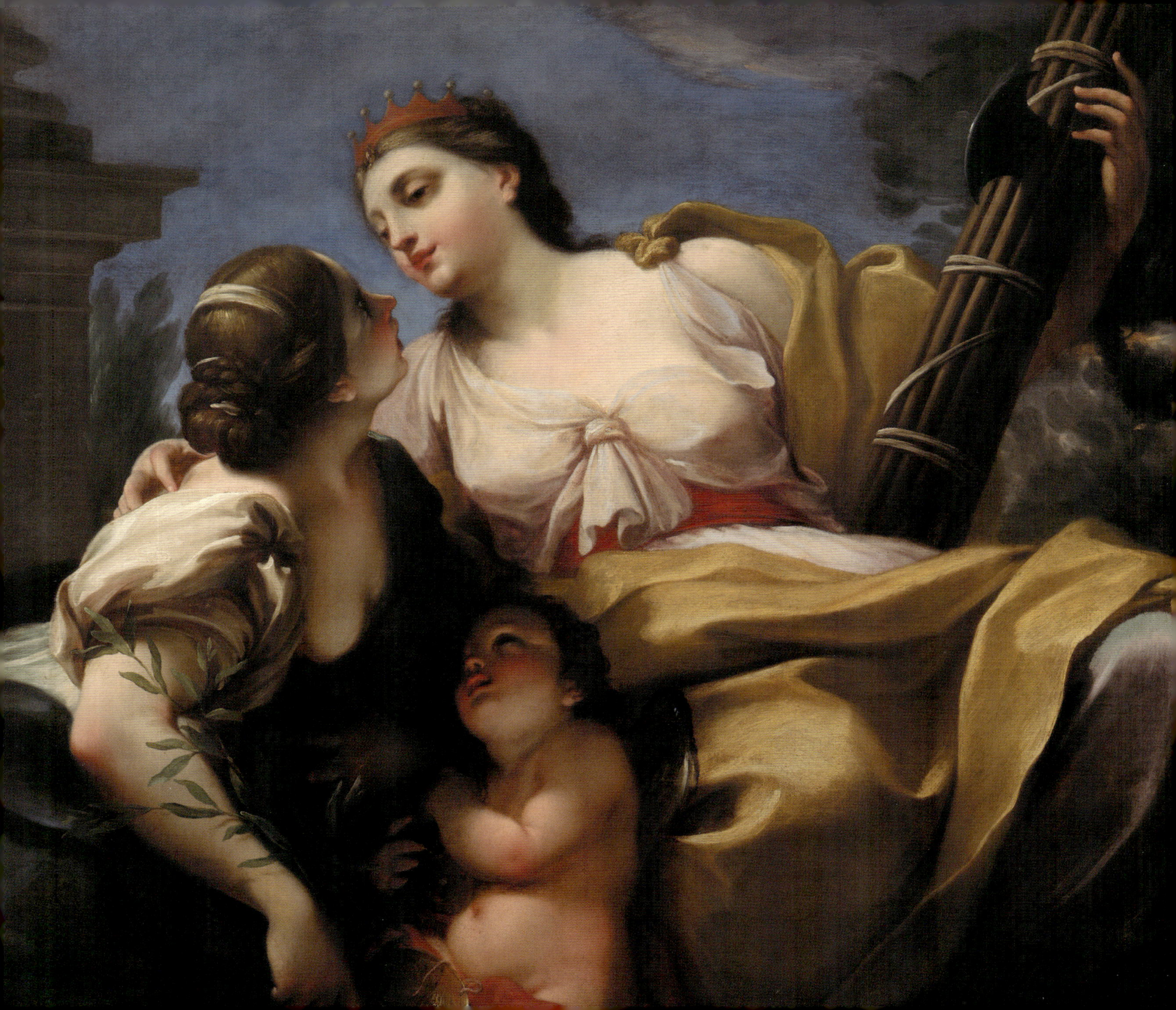

Even works of art which make political statements can be attractive. The figure on the left represents Peace; she holds an olive branch and is accompanied by the god of Love, Cupid. Peace embraces the figure representing Justice, who holds fasces, a bundle of rods containing an axe blade. Fasces were originally carried by ancient Roman magistrates who held ultimate power over life and death.

deviated from the officially-held beliefs of the Roman Church. Art once again played an important role, by promoting an emotionally-charged approach to religious belief.

The artistic period called the Baroque often featured extremes, both of style and mood, and proved to be the perfect medium for the promotion of this ideal. The depiction of saints undergoing tortuous trials which led to their martyrdom, or dramatically vivid images of biblical events, made compulsive – if sometimes repulsive – viewing. These artworks both terrorized and, rather perversely, even attracted some of those who may have been tempted to stray from the established Church.

For most of the eighteenth century various areas of Italy were affected politically by events connected to the complex succession of the Austrian branch of the Habsburg monarchy. The Grand Tour, usually an extended stay in the major cities of Italy by young aristocrats accompanied by companions or tutors, was a major feature of the period. This influx of well-off visitors provided a perfect opportunity for talented artists and business-minded art dealers to make a good living, as many of the visitors were seeking decorative works of art to take home.

During the 1790s French troops, under Napoleon Bonaparte, defeated the Austrians and invaded Italy. Many famous artworks were looted and taken to

'... the "Baroque" often featured extremes ...'

France. Artists' conscious revival of both the style and subject matter of classical art was particularly apt as the ambitious would-be emperor gradually worked his way through the country.

The early years of the nineteenth century were still dominated by foreign rule, but by the mid-century – as in other European countries – calls for revolution and independence were brewing. By the end of the century the inspirational military leader Giuseppe Garibaldi (1807–82) had played an important role in a complex series of events which resulted in Italy at last becoming a united country.

Luckily, most of the original art still survives; some of it in Italy, some of it scattered world-wide.

The Roman Catholic Church was all powerful in Italy. Clement VII (Pope from 1523–34) was a member of the Medici family, originally bankers, who ruled Florence from the fifteenth to the eighteenth century. This portrait, of which several copies survive, would have been an 'official image' of the pope.

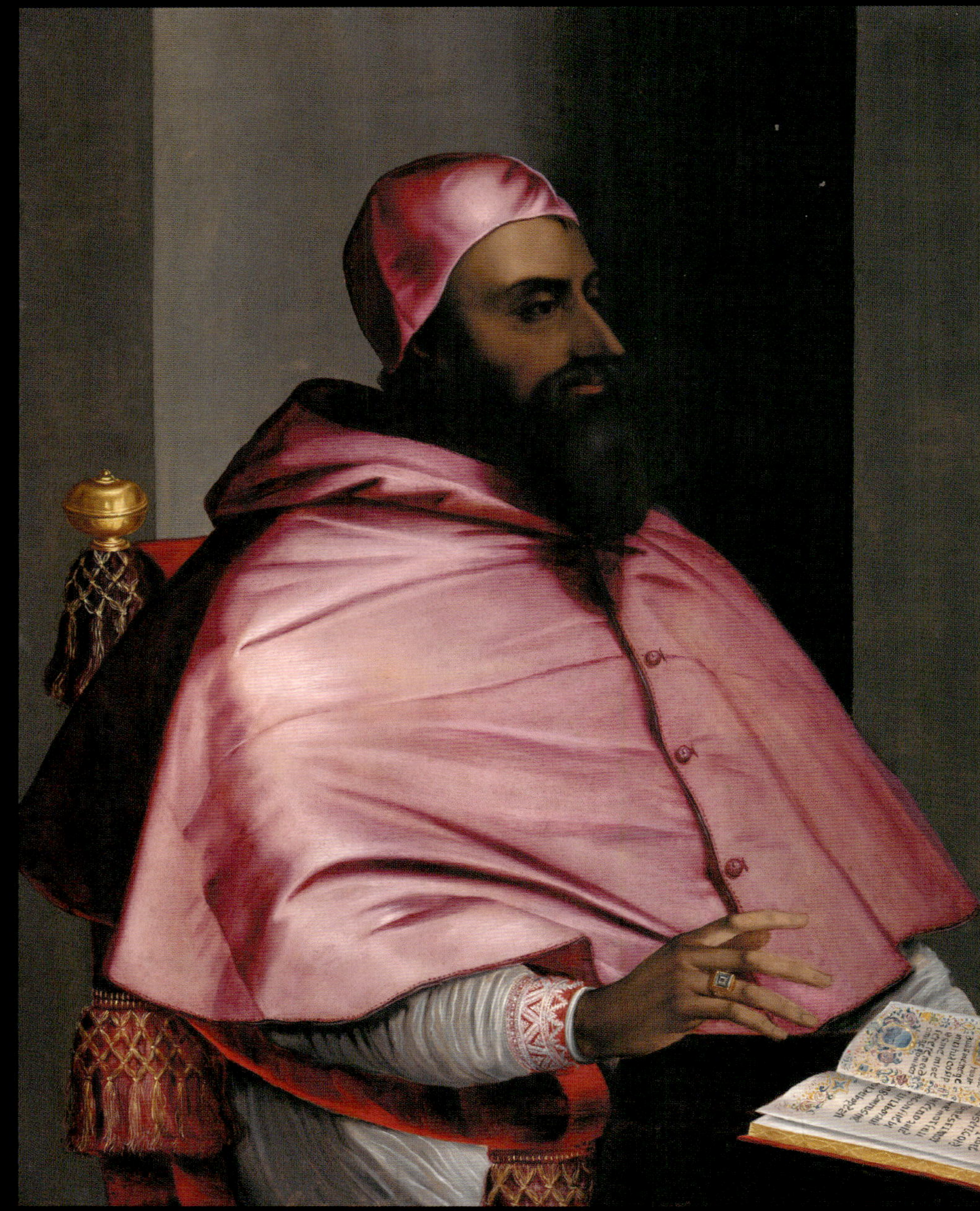

Giuseppe Garibaldi, 1883
Orazio Andreoni

Garibaldi was an inspirational leader viewed as a hero in Italy and beyond. This sculpture is said to have belonged to a Mrs Wallace 'who was an avid Garibaldian'. She was the sister of Sir Charles Tennant, Bart., who donated the sculpture to Glasgow's collection in 1902.

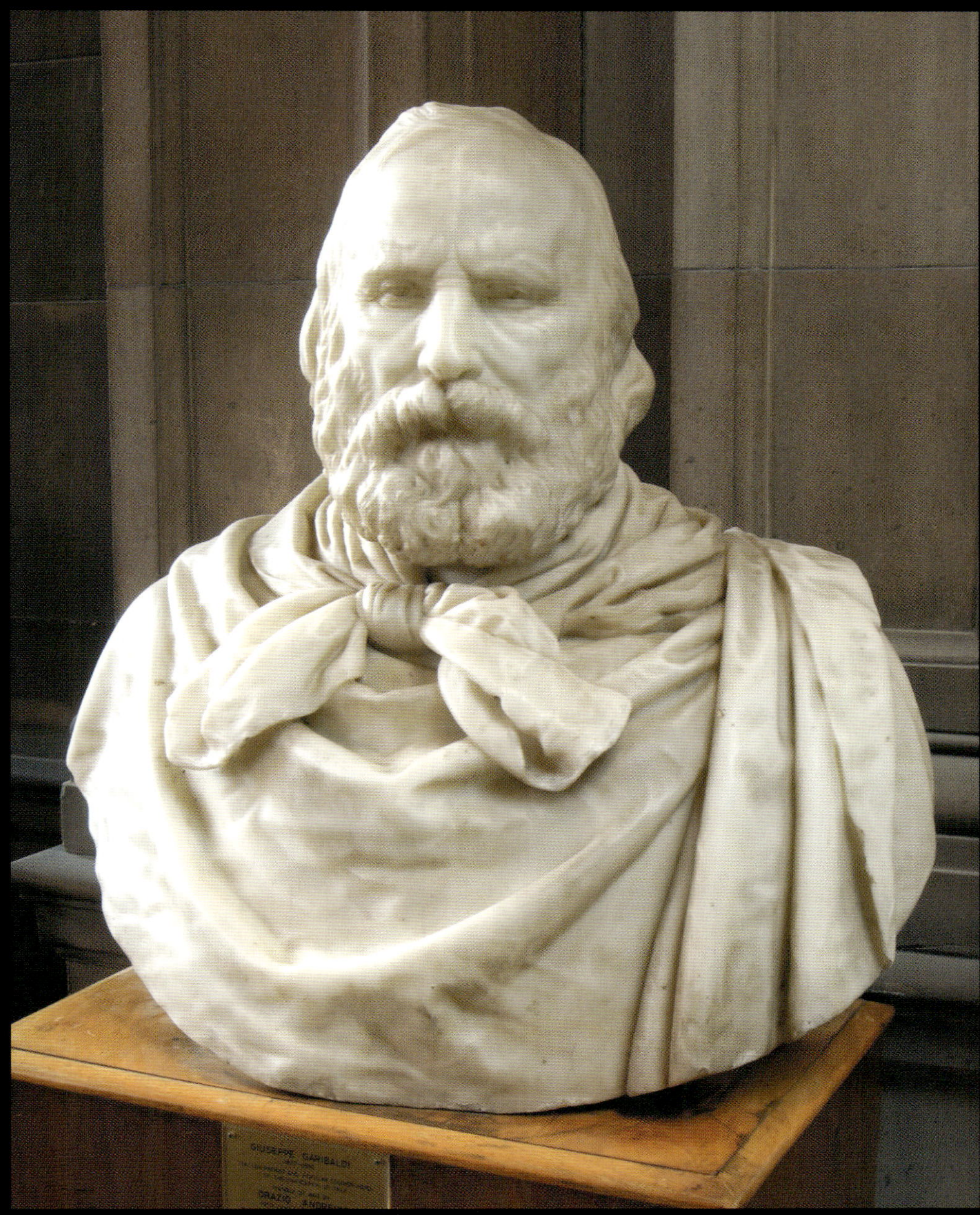

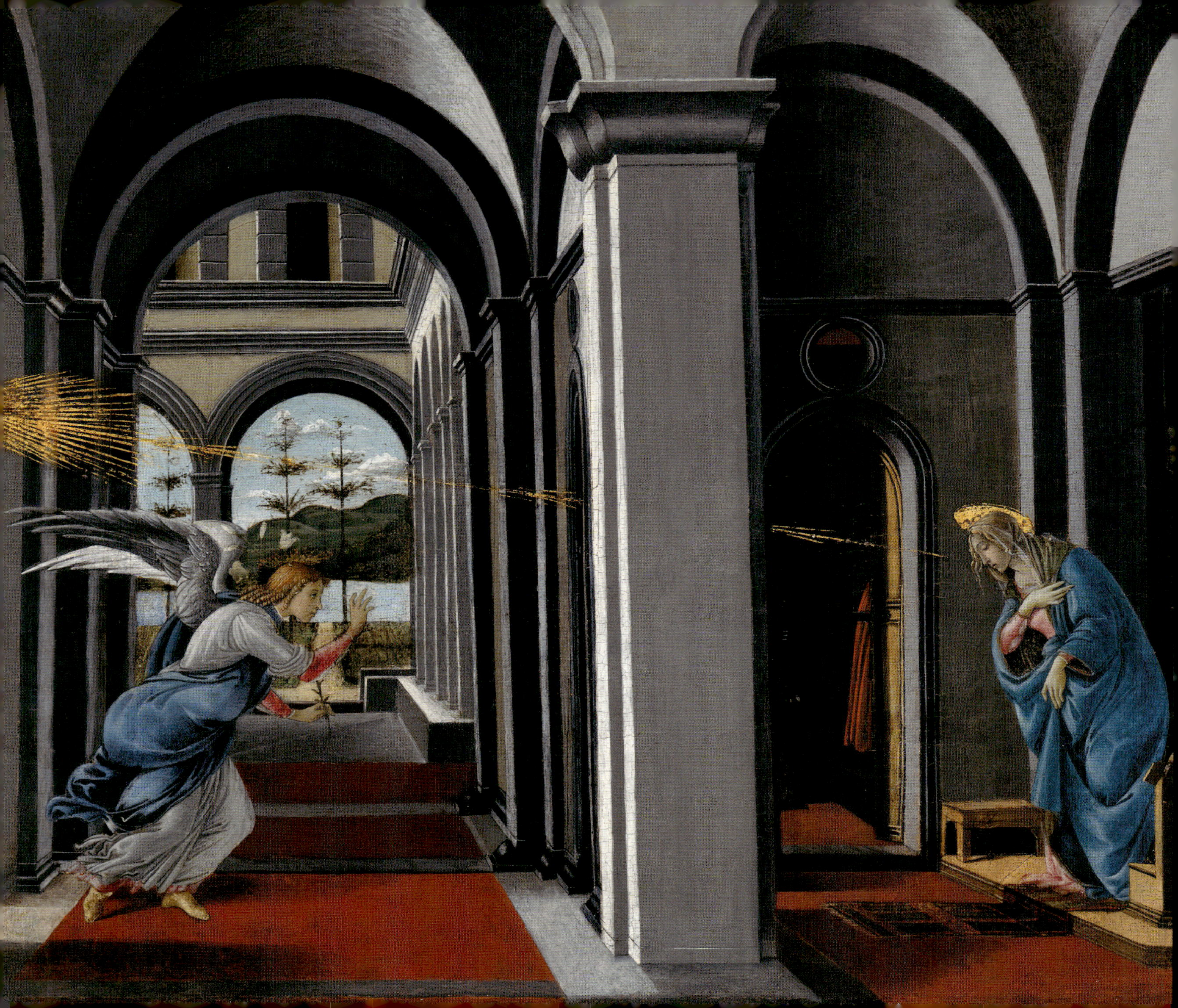

TRADITION AND INNOVATION
In Late Medieval Italy

Both in homes and in churches, art depicting scenes of Christ's life were the most favoured images during the fourteenth and fifteenth centuries. The annunciation of Christ's arrival in the Virgin Mary's body, his birth, and the lamentation over his dead body; all provided a strong emotional focus for both public and private prayer and meditation.

Individual saints, whose names were commonly given to people, offered devotional aids on a more personal level. Images of the infant Christ held by his mother were the most popular subject.

In purely artistic terms, this was a truly momentous period. Creation of illusory three-dimensional space by means of geometrical perspective developed in parallel with vividly convincing depictions of airy, distant landscapes. Some artists studied anatomy – even dissecting corpses – through which they learned how to depict three-dimensional human bodies. Non-religious subject-matter, from pre-Christian ages, began to appear as people's interest in ancient literature grew by way of the newly-invented printing presses.

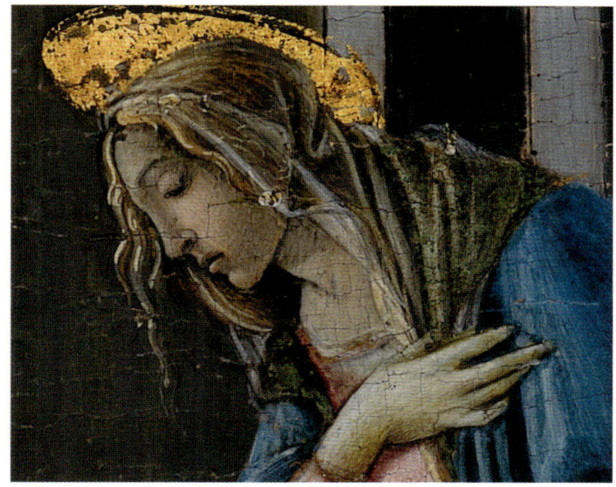

Overleaf left:
St Catherine Crowned,
c.1520
Bartolomeo Veneto

The spiked wheel in the corner identifies this richly-dressed girl as St Catherine of Alexandria, but instead of a halo of golden light she wears a crown of delicate jasmine flowers.

Overleaf right:
The Judgement of Paris,
c.1450–55
The Paris Master

Paris, Prince of Troy, presents a golden apple to Venus. He has chosen her as the most beautiful of these three goddesses. Inspired by classical Greek literature, this painting shows an important change. Religious topics gave ground to a wider range of subject as the Renaissance gathered momentum.

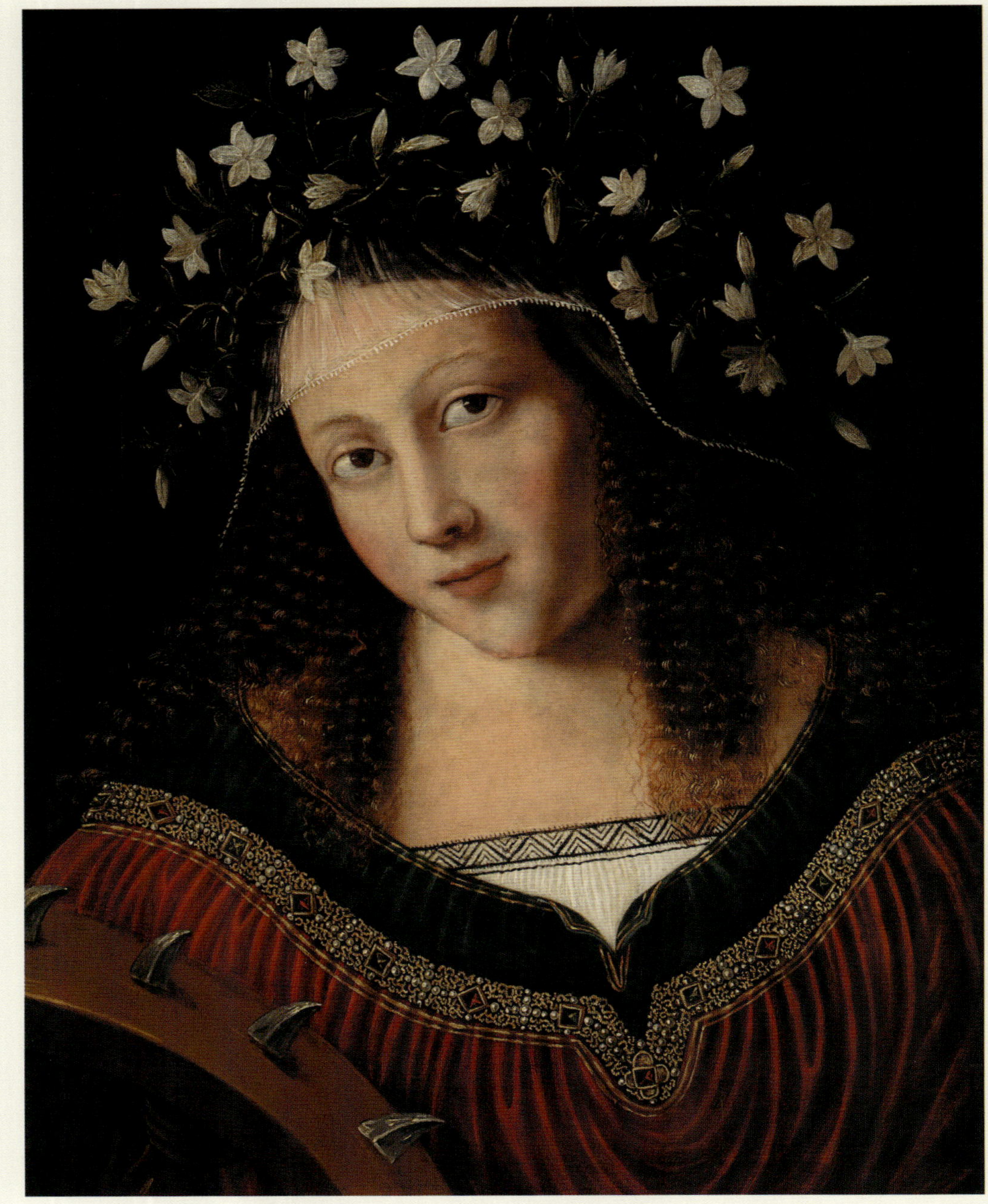

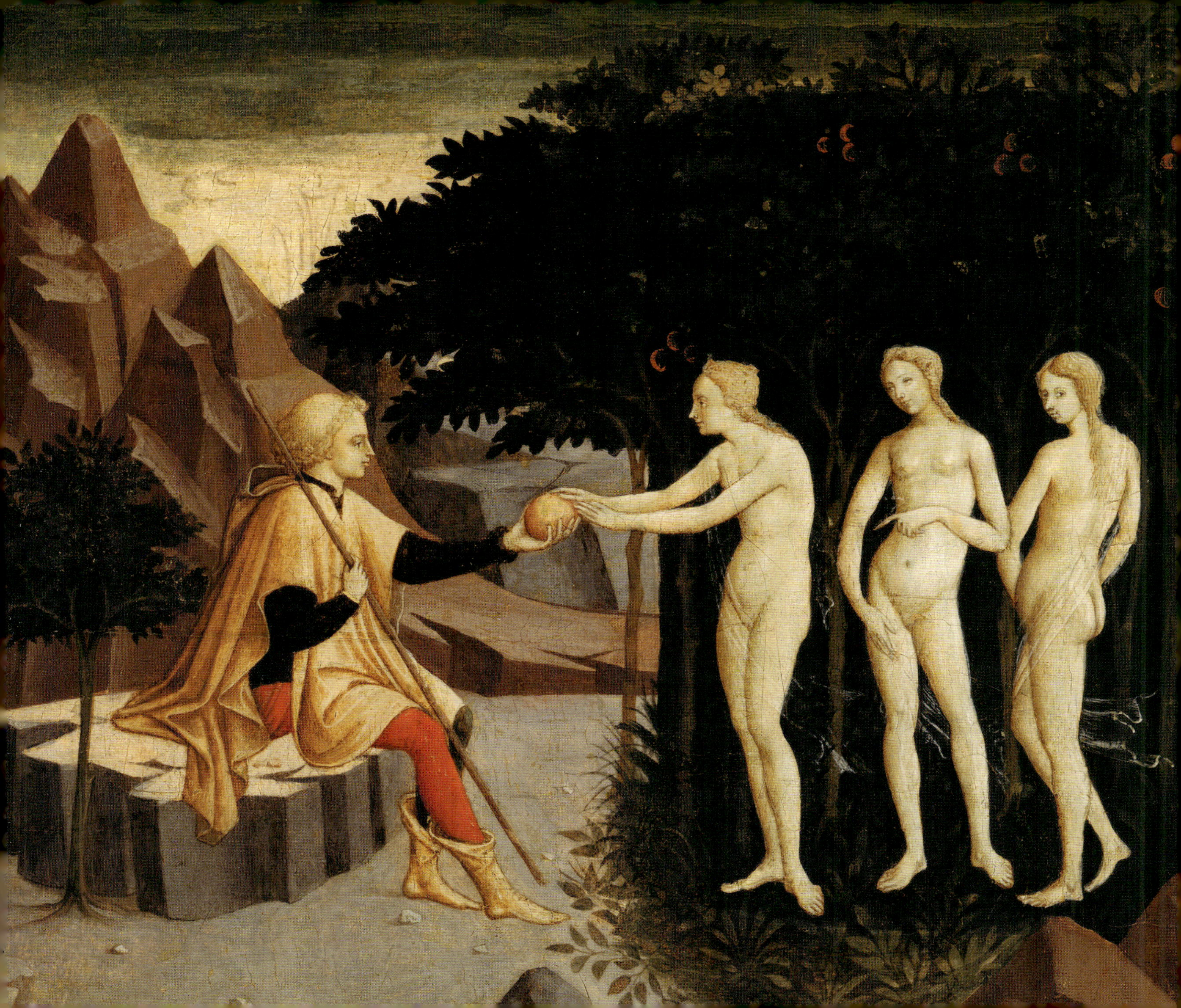

PATRONAGE AND POWER:
Tuscan art

St John the Baptist was patron saint of Florence, so this circular painting (*tondo*) would have been very fashionable. St John and the Christ Child embrace in gentle acknowledgment of the painfully important missions that each of them are destined to fulfil.

Florence, one of the richest and culturally most important cities during the late medieval period, is generally accepted as the hub around which Renaissance art developed and spread. The bank owned by the Medici family, influential Florentines, was the most important in Europe. The family effectively ruled the city during the fifteenth and sixteenth centuries.

Patronage was all-important to talented and ambitious artists, who relied on commissions from wealthy individuals or organizations. The Medici were quick to recognize and exploit local talent, for their own private commissions and for religious and urban projects. The most famous artists who worked in Florence were Michelangelo and Leonardo da Vinci, but the careers of many others were helped as a result of patronage by and on behalf of the Medici, other important Florentine families and religious institutions.

Alessandro Filipepi, known as Sandro Botticelli, was particularly favoured by the Medici family. Two of his most famous works, *Primavera* and *The Birth of Venus*, were Medici commissions, now in the Uffizi in Florence. Botticelli was taught by a popular Florentine artist, Filippo Lippi, whose son Filippino also became a painter. The works of Botticelli, Filippino Lippi, and Lippi's pupil Raffaellino del Garbo, have often been confused, as their styles are similar. Art historians have unravelled many mistaken attributions. This painting has previously been attributed to Botticelli and Lippi in turn!

Other Tuscan towns claim fine artists among their inhabitants (though many artists sooner or later moved into cities, where opportunities were much greater). Siena rivalled Florence, and was large enough to support its own body of artists, who worked in a recognizably Sienese style. Luca Signorelli was from Cortona in southern Tuscany, and probably trained nearby. He was already familiar with the style of artists working in Florence by the time he undertook a commission for the Pope in Rome in his early thirties, so had clearly travelled around his home region.

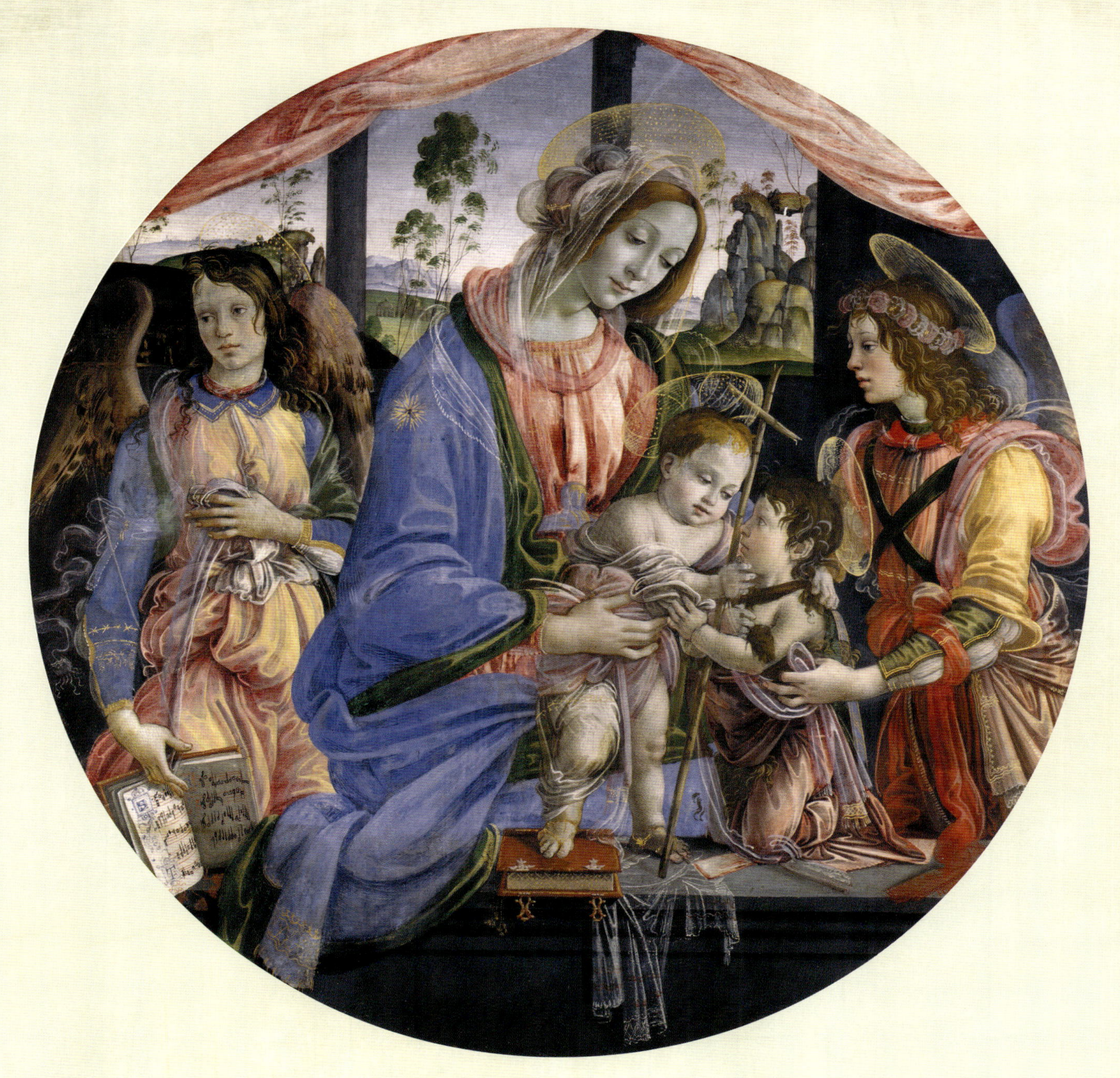

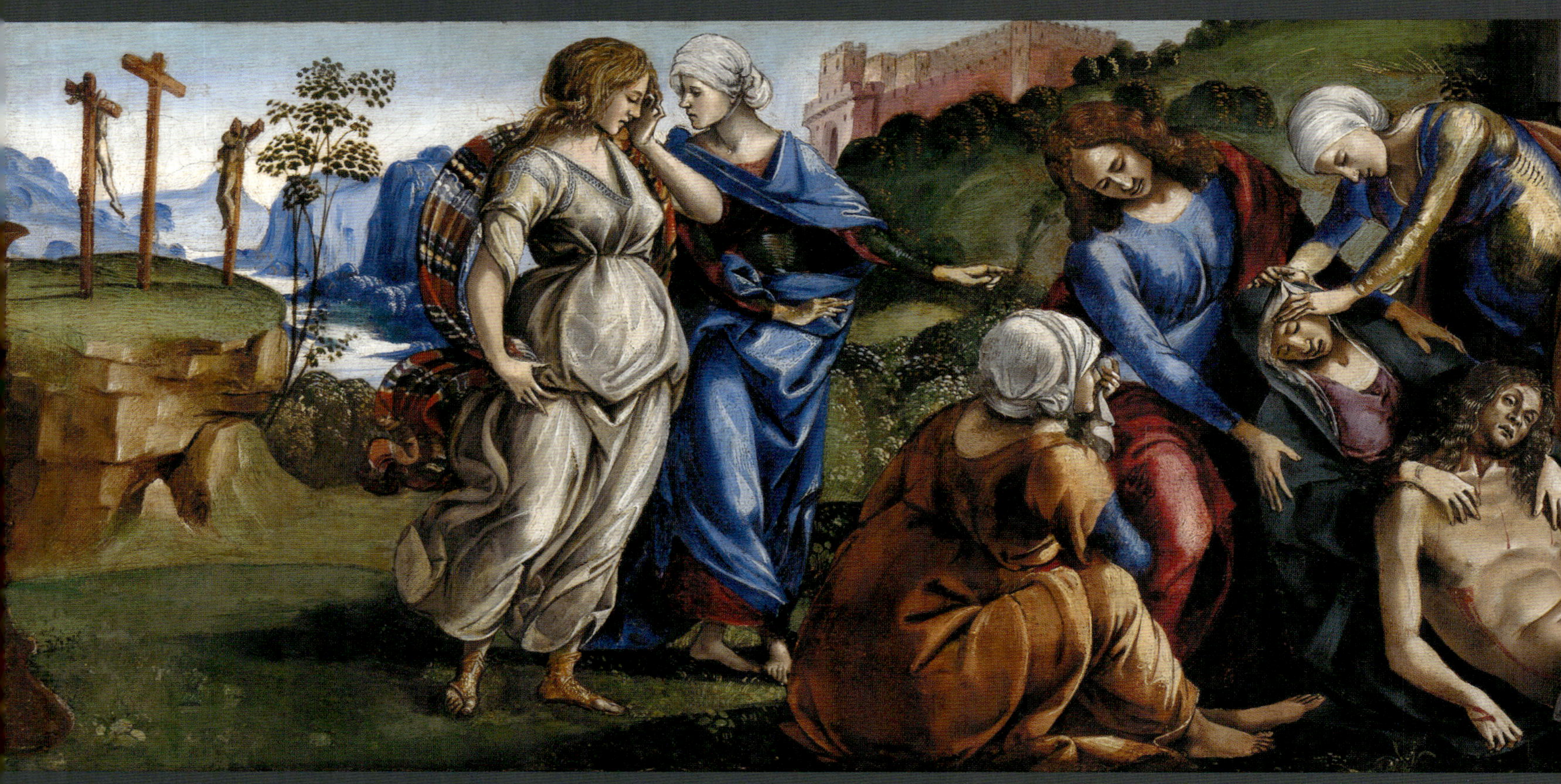

Lamentation Over the Dead Christ, c.1488–90
Luca Signorelli

Predella panels formed the lowest part of large-scale altarpieces. The horizontal format could have looked awkward, but Signorelli has cleverly exploited this shape by stretching out the body of Christ. His pose is echoed by the grief-stricken mourners behind him in the central group.

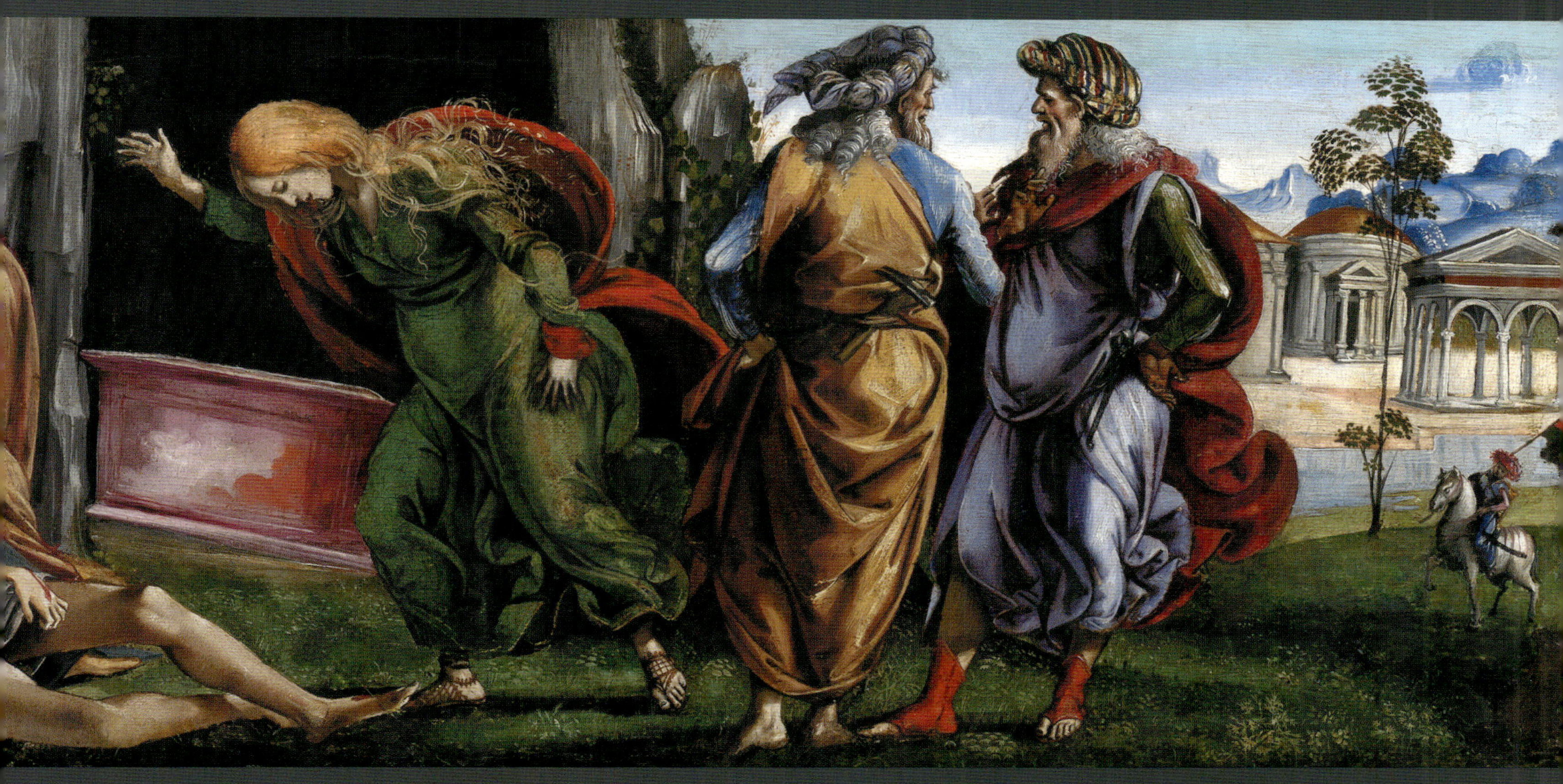

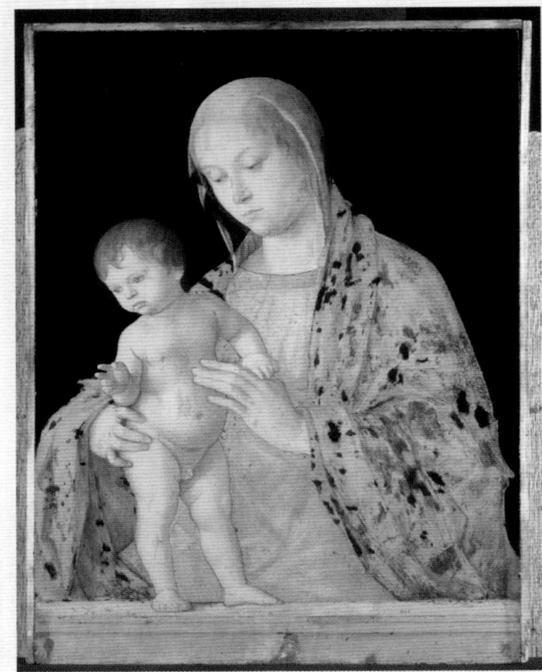

An infrared reflectogram showing the black background.

Giovanni Bellini specialized in producing **beautiful paintings showing the Madonna and Christ Child, often alone – as in both paintings shown here – but sometimes accompanied by saints.**

The earlier painting shows the Madonna gently supporting the Christ Child, who blesses the faithful. It was hung fairly high up – the original viewer probably knelt in prayer – so the downward glances of both the Madonna and Christ were directed towards the supplicant. This establishes an extremely intimate link between the image and viewer.

Infrared reflectography and x-radiography suggest that the artist painted the plain dark background as we see it now. Bellini often made a dramatic feature of the contrast between a solid black ground and the gentle flesh tones of the figures, set against the bright fabrics which enrich their appearance.

The later painting was owned by an eminent Italian family, the Barberini, for around 300 years. The exact meaning of the floral sprig held on a fine thread by Christ is not clear, but the Madonna is holding her hand beneath the sprig, ready to catch it if it falls, offering a clue. In religious literature Christ was often referred to as 'the final flowering' of the Tree of Jesse (a religious family tree, based on his supposed Old Testament ancestry), so the sprig possibly represents his own connection to that tree. In art, both Christ and the Madonna traditionally have foreknowledge of the future, so here they meditate on Christ's future death on the cross.

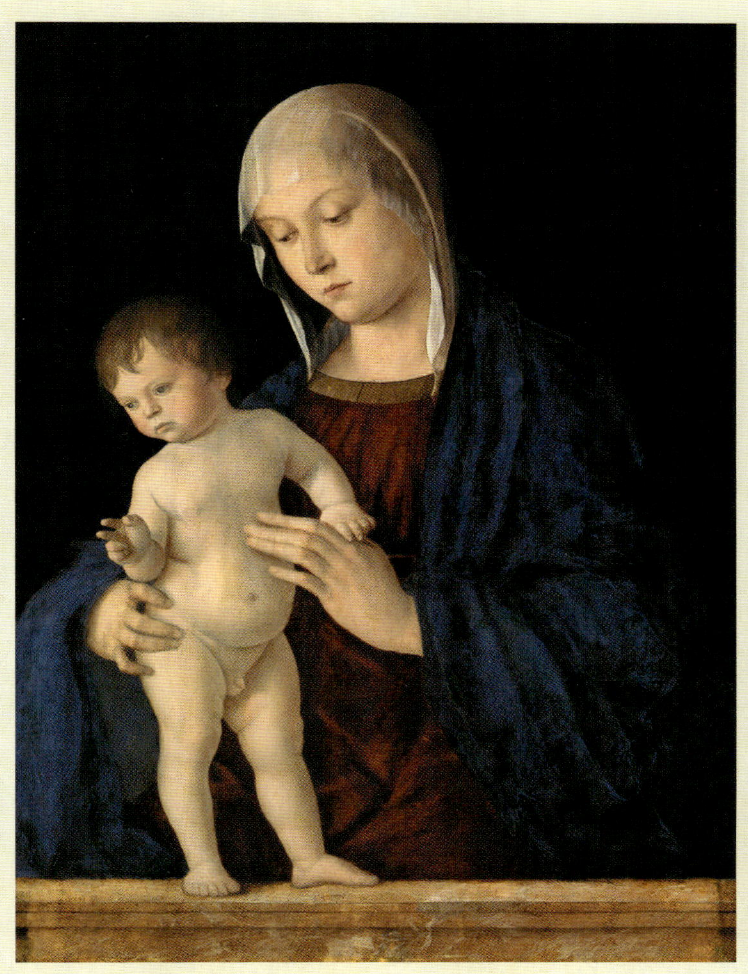

Madonna and Child, c.1480–5
Giovanni Bellini

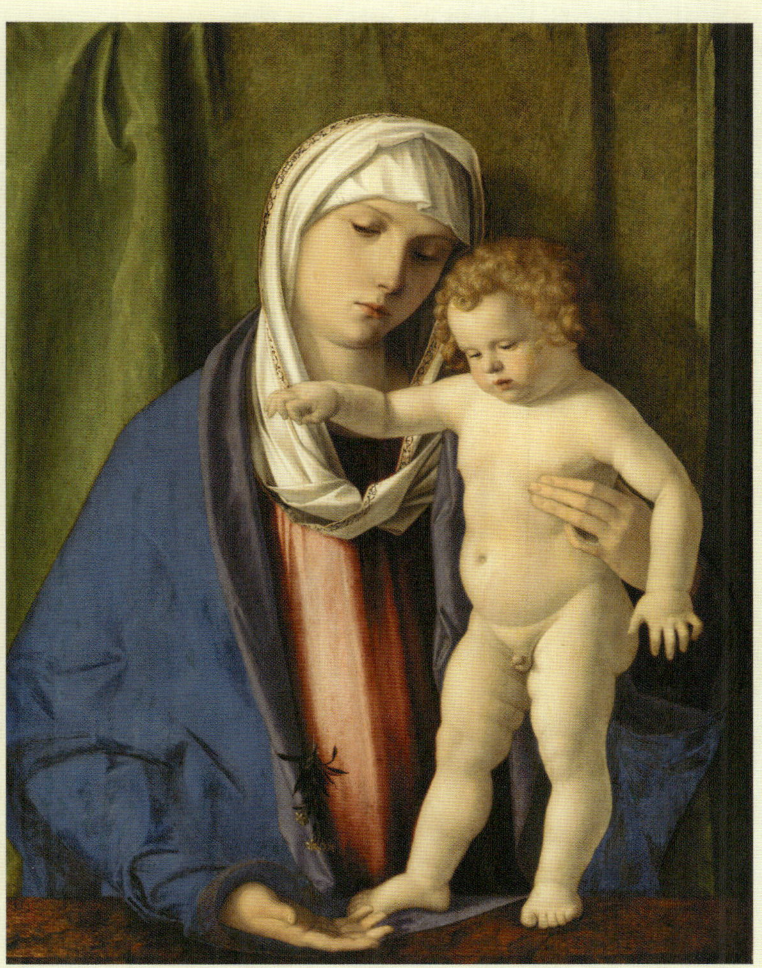

Madonna and Child, c.1485–8
Giovanni Bellini

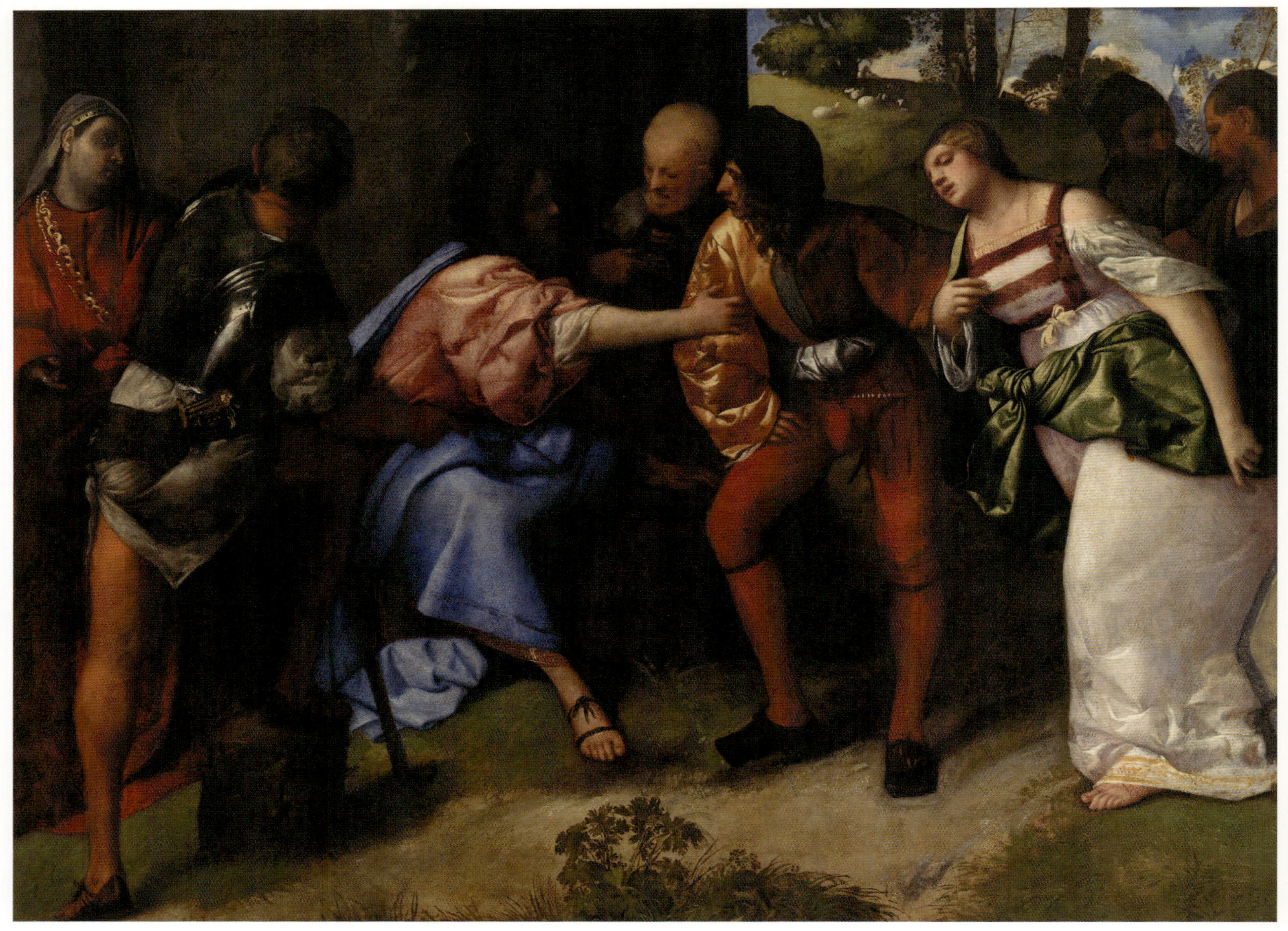

16TH-CENTURY SPLENDOUR:
Renaissance art

Paintings from the sixteenth century mark a turning point in the technique and subject matter adopted by newly-ambitious painters. The style of paintings changed quite radically.

Figures became more solid in appearance, influenced by artists' study of anatomy and rediscovered classical sculptures, which were often of nude figures. The surroundings in which the figures were placed became softer and more atmospheric and an increasingly confident use of oil paint led to richer, gleaming layers of colour.

Many artists working later in the century painted work of a rather different nature. They refined and elongated figures' limbs, and experimented with complex poses (to show off their knowledge of anatomy) and rainbow-hued colours. This consciously elegant style was known as Mannerism.

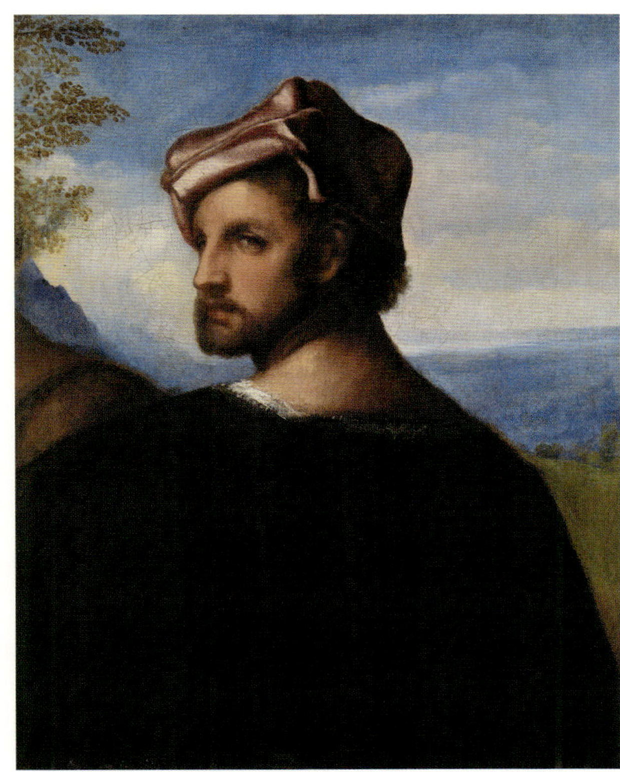

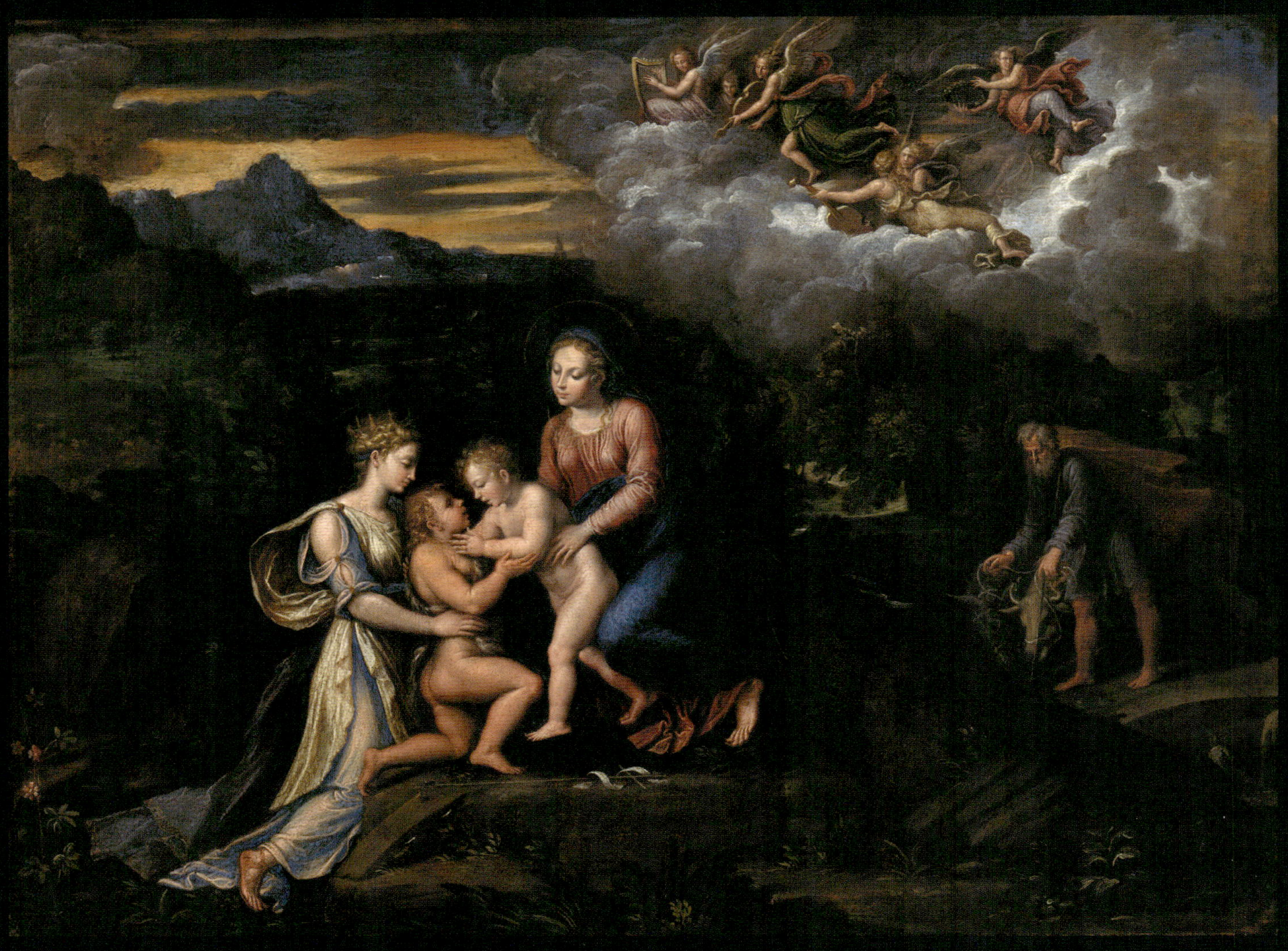

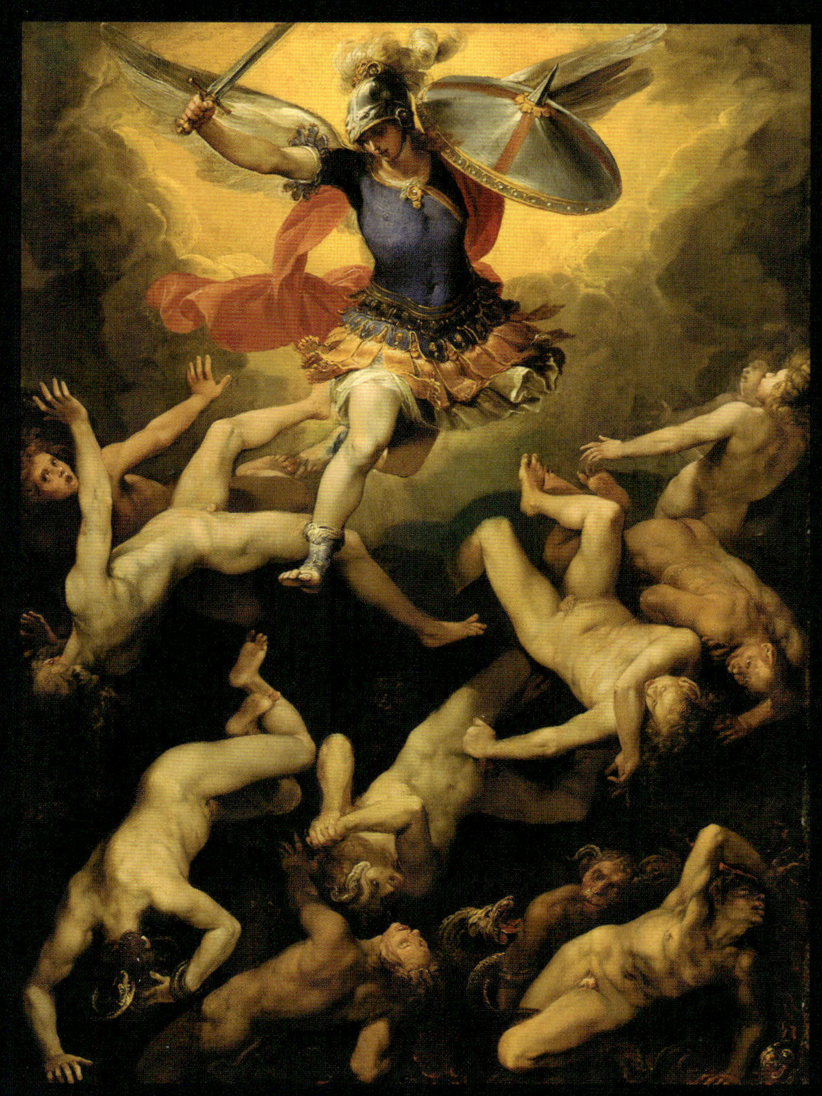

Left:
***Virgin and Child in a Landscape with the Child Baptist and St Catherine of Alexandria**, c.1545*
Girolamo da Carpi

The early Christian martyr St Catherine of Alexandria, famous for having broken the wheel on which she was tortured before being beheaded, presents the infant St John the Baptist to the Christ Child. St Catherine is said to have dreamed that she married Jesus.

Right:
***The Archangel Michael and the Rebel Angels**,*
c.1592–3
Cavaliere D'Arpino

This image, painted on metal, vividly demonstrates most elements of the later-Renaissance style called Mannerism. The figures are shown in complex poses, which show off the artist's anatomical knowledge. As St Michael enters in a brilliantly-lit flourish, the evil angel Lucifer and his followers tumble headlong into Hell.

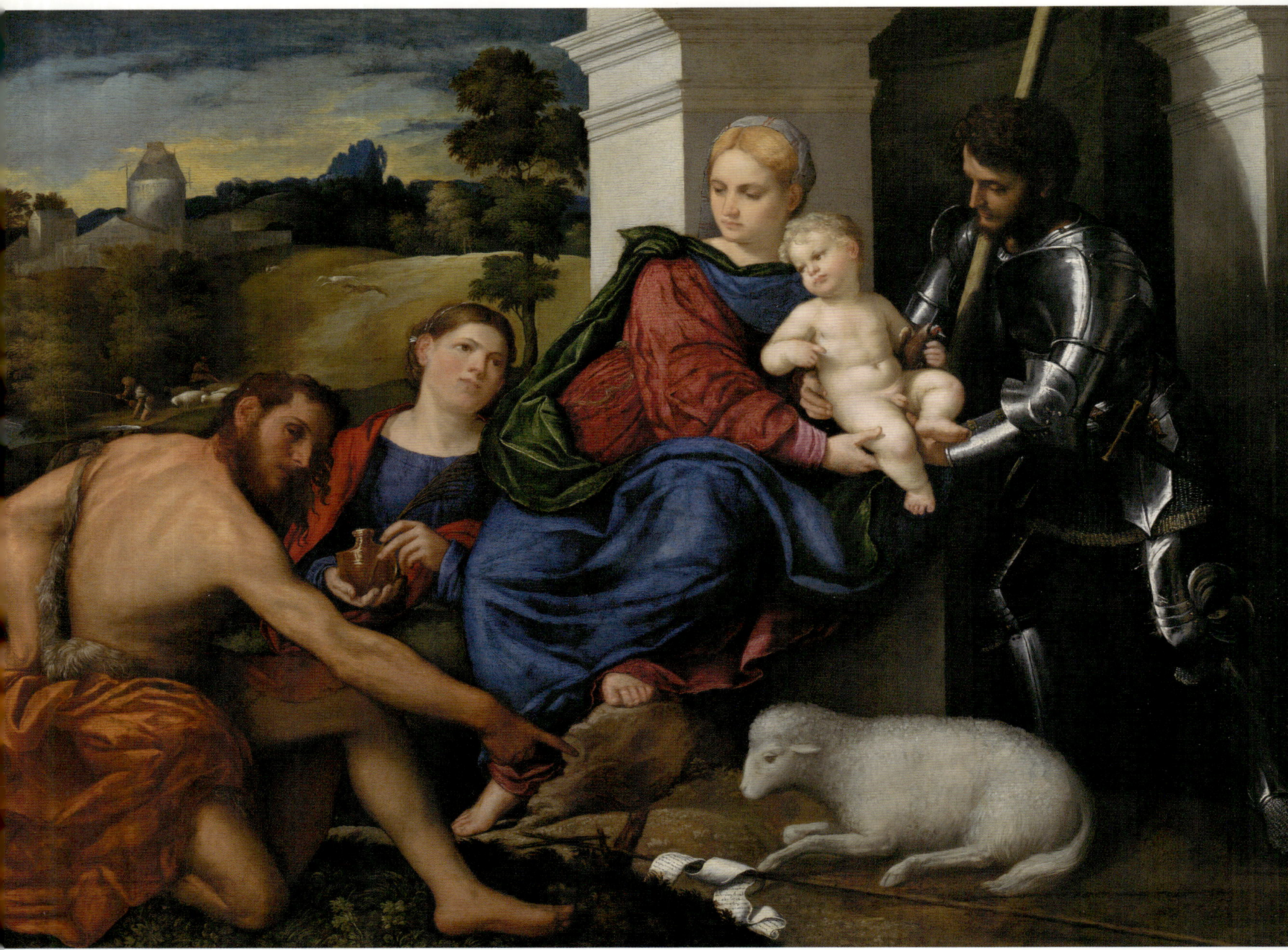

ARTISTIC INNOVATORS:
Venetian Renaissance art

Left:
Madonna and Child with Saints John the Baptist, Mary Magdalen and George?, c.1524
Paris Bordon

This bold, diagonal composition is typical of the large-scale holy figure group. The atmospheric dawning sky, the fisherman, shepherd and sheep can be interpreted as symbols of the Christian faith.

Venice was – and is – a very special place. Both the watery city and the surrounding region are picturesque in all senses of the word, as demonstrated by later artists such as Canaletto and Guardi. However, during the medieval and Renaissance periods Venice was best known as a thriving port, linking east and west via both sea and land routes. Rich fabrics, precious pigments and exotic artefacts all passed into and through the city.

The main change in painting technique during the Renaissance was the increasing use of oil (rather than egg) as a binding medium for pigments. The use of oil was adopted at an early stage in Venice, with stunning results. Instead of rather matt, chalky-like shades, the new technique resulted in rich glowing colours. These could be applied thickly, to give texture, or as oil-rich delicate glazes, piled one upon another to provide the glossy, glowing effects of light.

The Bellini family and their students dominated the world of Venetian painting for many years. The long-lived and renowned Giovanni Bellini taught the two major Venetian painters of the next generation, Giorgione and Titian. Titian himself then taught and influenced many more painters, including Paris Bordon, during his own long life.

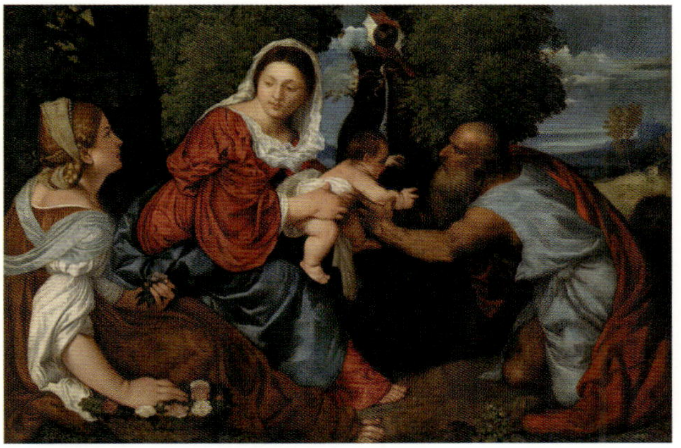

Madonna and Child with Saints Jerome and Dorothy, c.1520
Francesco Vecellio

As Francesco worked in a similar style, paintings – like this one – have often been mistakenly attributed to his famous brother, Titian. The finely-painted figure of St Jerome, on the right, is in stark contrast to the much less fine St Dorothy, seated on the left. Experts consider that St Jerome may actually have been painted by Titian himself.

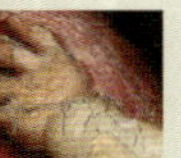

Works in Focus

Bordon painted this work about two years before his *Madonna and Child with Saints John the Baptist, Mary Magdalen and George?* The subject matter is similar but the style is softer, and the mood more gentle. It brings to mind the atmospheric work of Giorgione, who, as both artists' biographer Giorgio Vasari wrote, was much admired by Bordon.

However, the painting as it is seen now is not how it appeared when bequeathed by Mrs John Graham Gilbert in 1877. Then, the kneeling figure on the left was clothed – like St Anthony Abbot next to him – in a friar's rough habit. It was only when the painting was photographed under infra-red light that it became apparent that the left-hand friar had been painted over another, totally different person. After discussion, the decision was made to remove the over-painted friar and reveal the original figure. The person who originally commissioned the painting (the donor), was identified in an early description of the work as a Dr Genova. The left-hand figure revealed, wearing richly-quilted silk, is almost certainly this Dr Genova, who is being presented to the Madonna and Child, encouraged by the two saints.

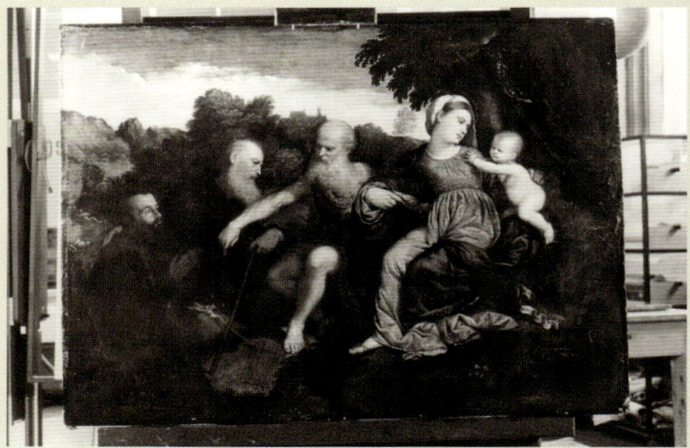

The painting, prior to cleaning in 1981.

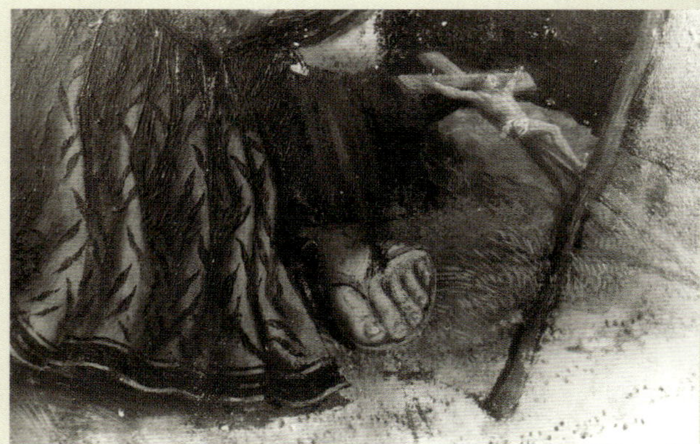

A detail of the foot.

One curiosity is the seemingly 'odd' foot wearing a sandal, just in front of the doctor. This foot, also revealed during the cleaning process, corresponds to one belonging to St Anthony Abbot in an almost identical painting made for another donor. Here it seems to have been moved out of its original place, thus making the saint's pose rather difficult to understand!

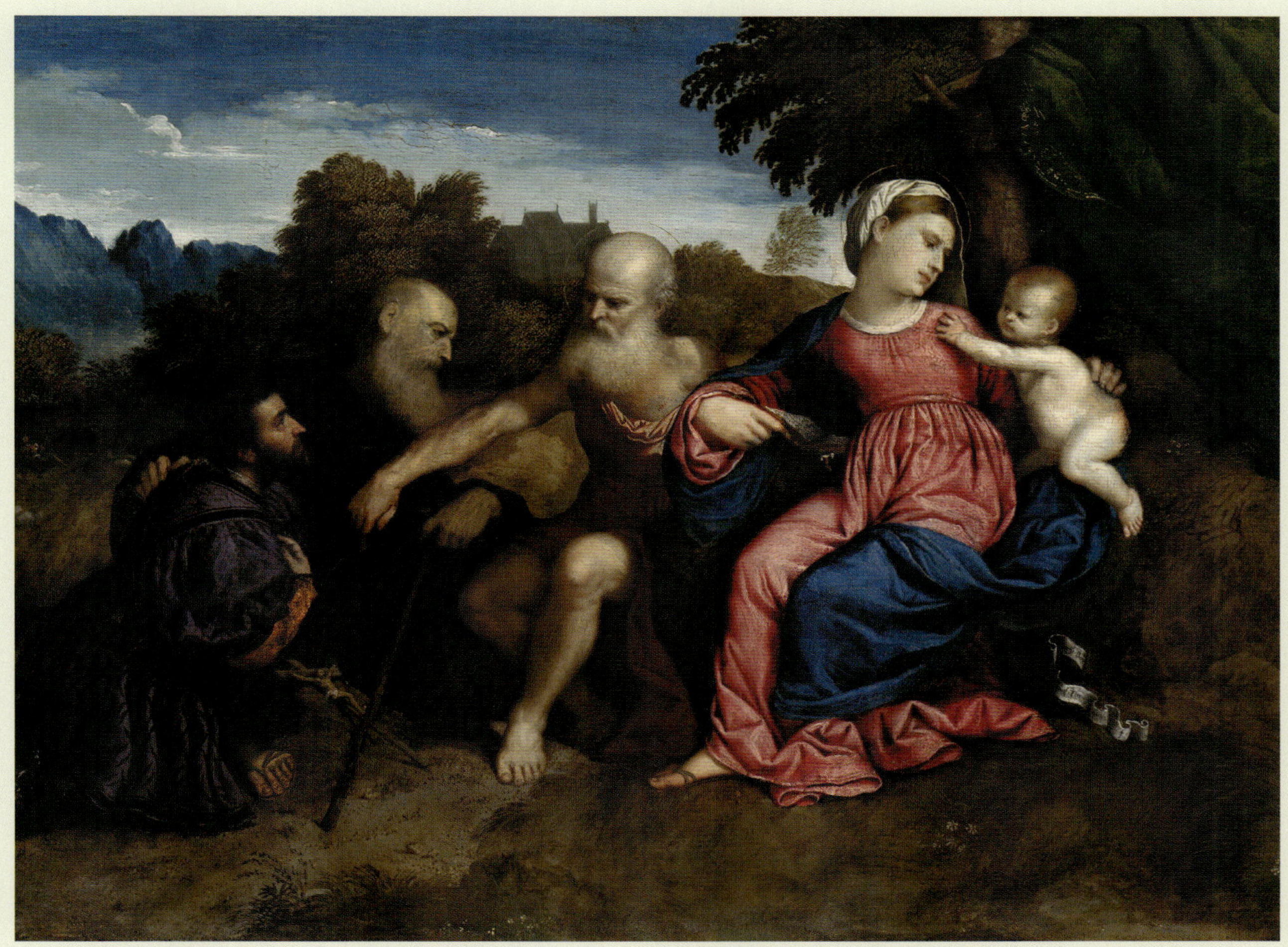

*Madonna and Child
with Saints Jerome,
Anthony Abbot and a
Donor*, c.1522
Paris Bordon

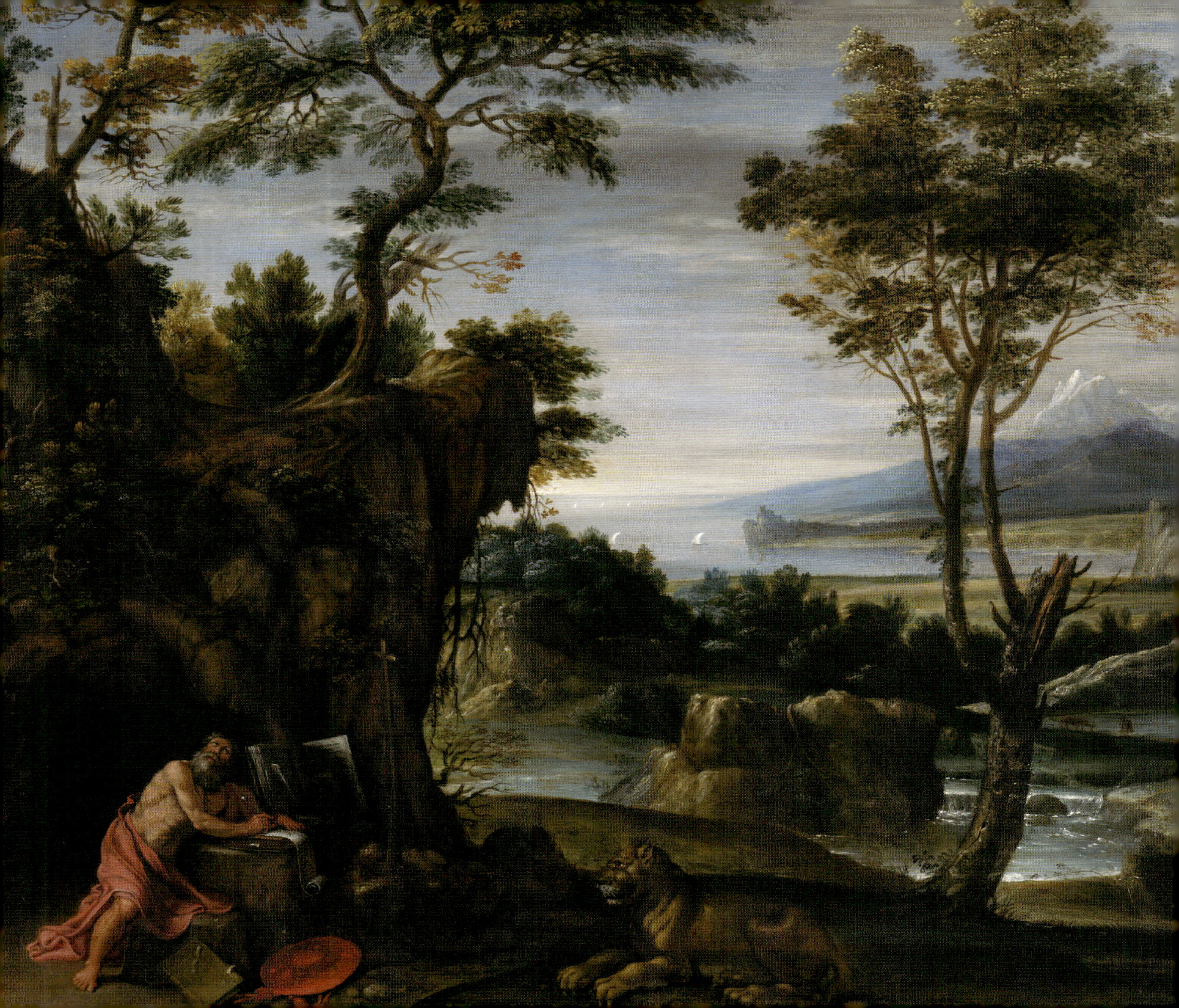

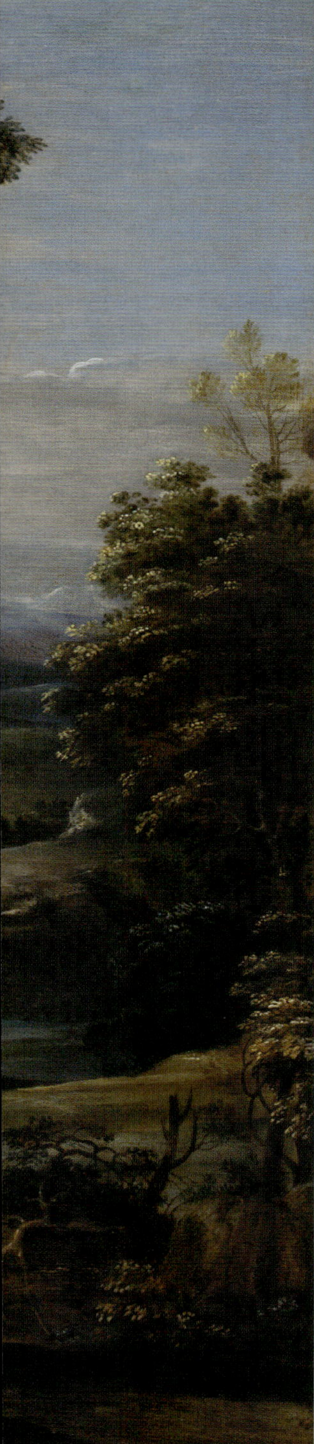

DIVERGENT PATHS:
Italian Baroque art

By the seventeenth century art was more dramatic in style. Art and architecture of the middle and latter part of the century is usually known as Baroque.

Baroque art is typified by the use of *chiaroscuro* – boldly contrasting light and shade – which heightens theatrical and emotional intensity; dynamic movement and the artist's use of diagonals contribute further to the drama.

At the same time, other artists were using different, rather more subtle, methods in their attempts to convey emotion. They created a serene atmosphere, featured glances rather than extravagant gestures, and suggested flowing movement rather than swirling intensity. These two methods of working overlapped to some degree, and elements of both can be found within a single painting – as in Dolci's *Salome*, where the harsh subject and dark background are softened by Salome's gentle expression and softly-depicted costume.

'… artists were using different methods …'

**Landscape with St Jerome, c.1610
Domenichino**

This painting shows how artists' subjects were changing. In contrast to previous practice, the saint and his attribute of a lion have been reduced in size and moved from centre-stage. The brilliantly composed atmospheric landscape is the main subject of the painting.

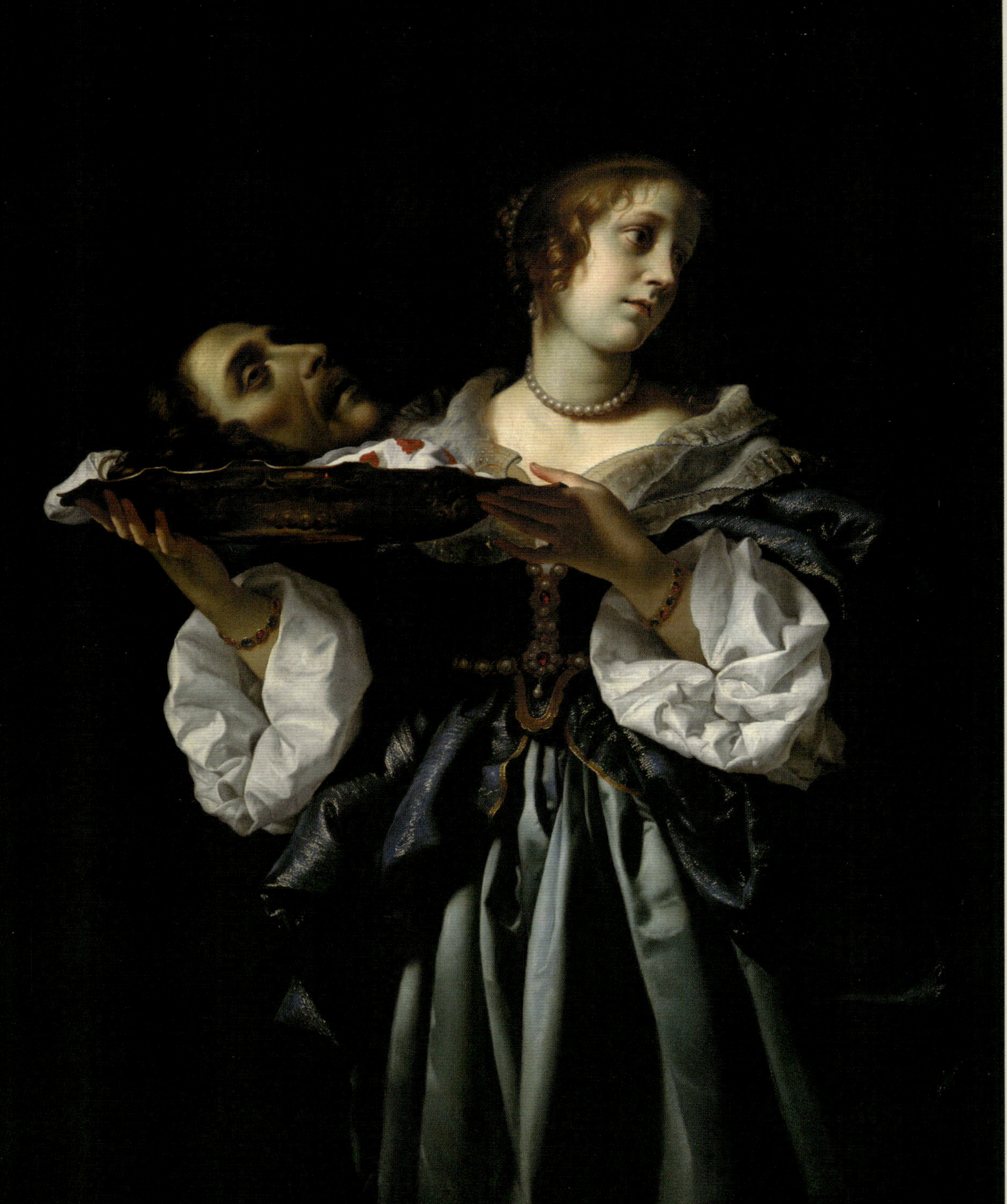

Salome with the Head of St John the Baptist, c.1681–5, Carlo Dolci

The beautiful, richly-dressed Salome has been enticed by her mother and stepfather into requesting the head of St John the Baptist. She carries his head, but looks away from it – perhaps seeking approval for her action.

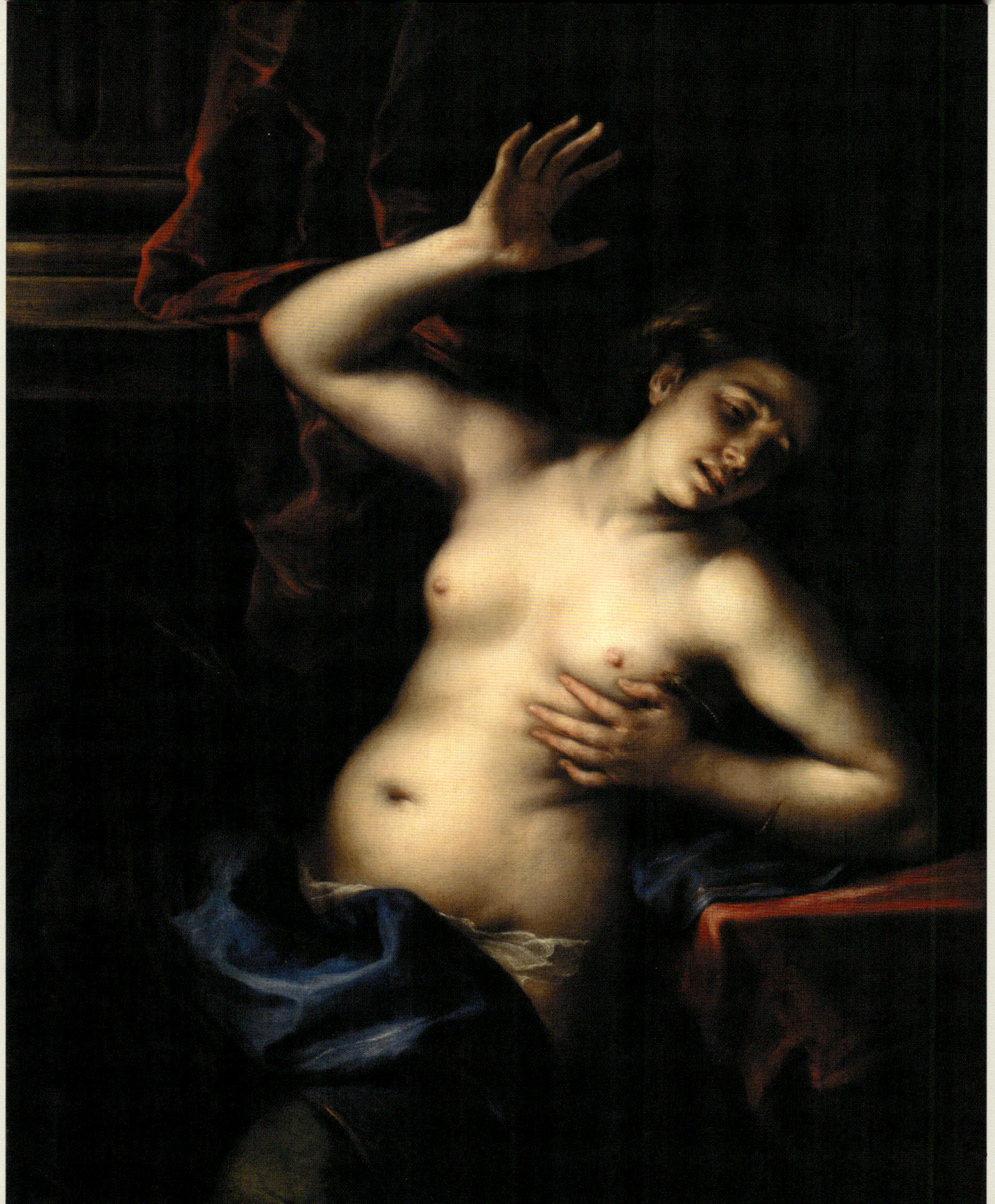

Death of Cleopatra,
*c.*1645–50
Francesco del Cairo

As in the painting of Salome, large-scale female figures – including nudes – were now becoming acceptable. Cleopatra is shown as both exotic and erotic; her nudity enhanced by the rich fabrics framing from her voluptuous figure.

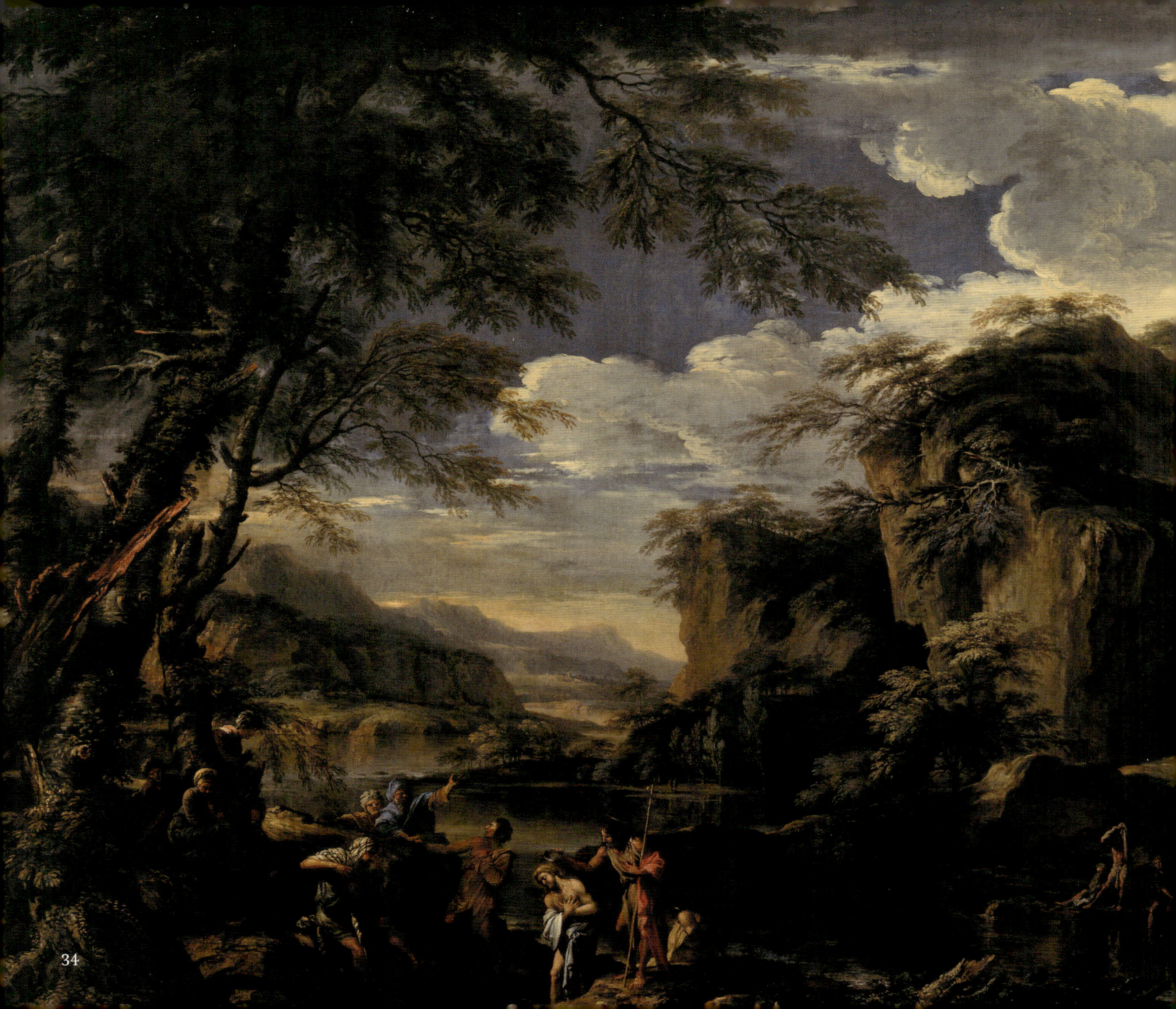

DRAMA AND DEVOTION:
Staged scenes

This is one of a pair of powerful landscapes commissioned in the mid-seventeenth century. This painting shows St John the Baptist baptizing Jesus while the companion painting shows him revealing Christ to the Disciples, an event which happened later. These paintings are considered Rosa's finest landscapes.

Both works initially appear similar, as they almost entirely consist of an overpoweringly moody landscape of rocky cliffs, gigantic trees, and distant misty mountains, all beneath a dramatically-lit sky. The actual subject is almost lost amid the massive background, but both elements are important. Rather than just illustrating the biblical scenes, Rosa has used the landscape elements symbolically, providing greater emotional depth. The rosy dawn light in the sky is particularly important, symbolizing both the formal beginning of Christ's ministry following his baptism and the subsequent spread of the Christian message.

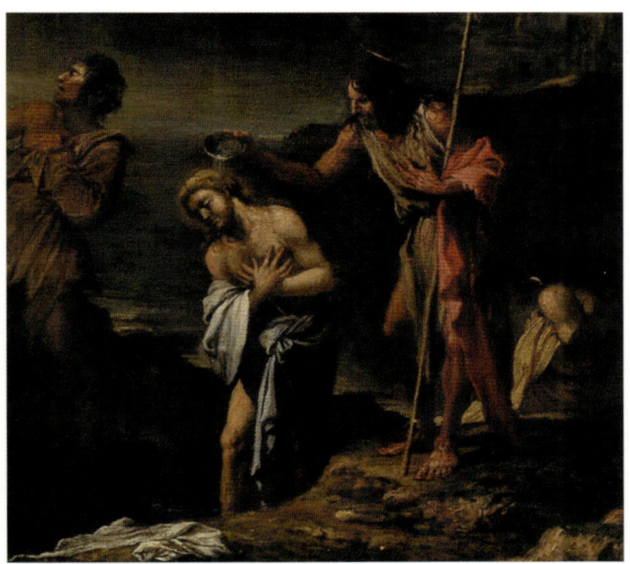

St John the Baptist Baptizing Christ in the River Jordan, 1656–7
Salvator Rosa

Works in Focus

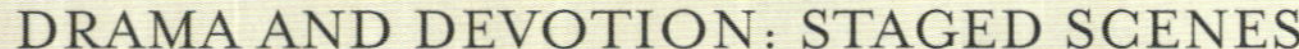

Although these two paintings initially look very similar, and their subjects are related, the styles used by their painters are rather different. These contrasting styles represent two different aspects of art of the Baroque period.

The painting by Sassoferrato shows a close-knit, statuesque group of figures which almost fills the entire space. The mood is gentle, the light subdued; only the gesture made by John the Baptist's mother, St Elizabeth, is disturbing. She has recognized that the seemingly innocent gesture of her son passively accepting the drink proffered by Jesus is a premonition of the Last Supper. The Madonna accepts this pre-knowledge more readily – she helps to support the drinking bowl.

In contrast, Grammatica's painting is rather like a dramatic stage set. Strong light from the left emphasizes the illusionistic depth and detail of both the setting and the figures. This, and

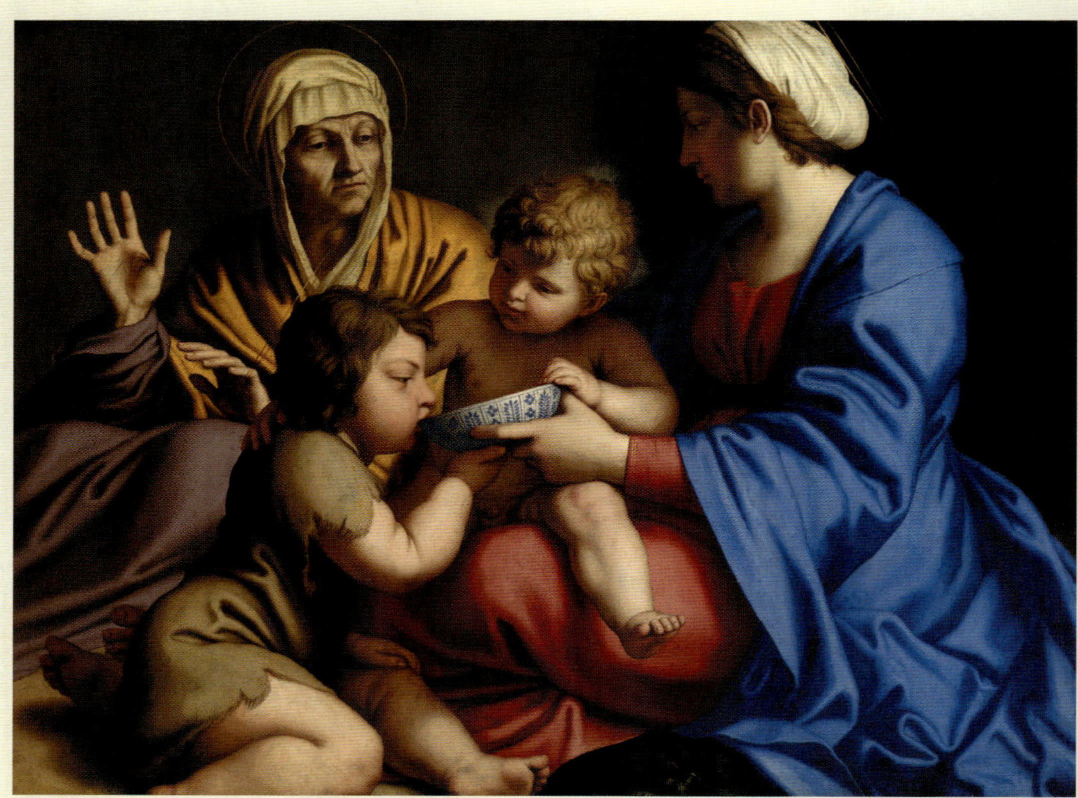

Madonna and Child with St Elizabeth and the Child Baptist, c.1640s
Giovanni Battista Salvi (Sassoferrato)

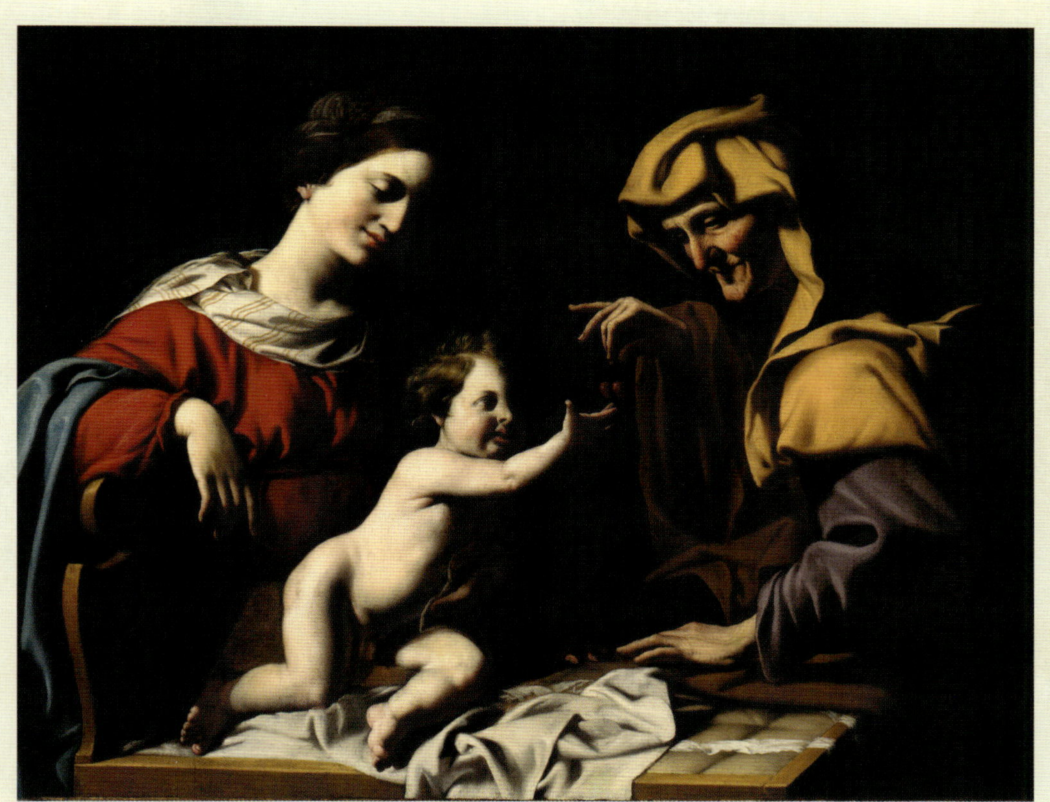

Madonna and Child with St Anne, c.1614–17
Anteveduto Grammatica

the heavily-accentuated realism of the old lady's face, makes the scene appear more life-like, less like a posed work of art. The iconographically crucial action between St Anne and the young Jesus is captured as if in suspended animation. She offers cherries, representing the forbidden fruit eaten by Adam and Eve, and red – like the blood he will shed – to Jesus. He eagerly reaches out for them, acknowledging by this action his acceptance of his destiny, to die in order to redeem believers from that original sin. His mother smiles, but looks thoughtful. As in Sassoferrato's painting, she knows what is going to happen.

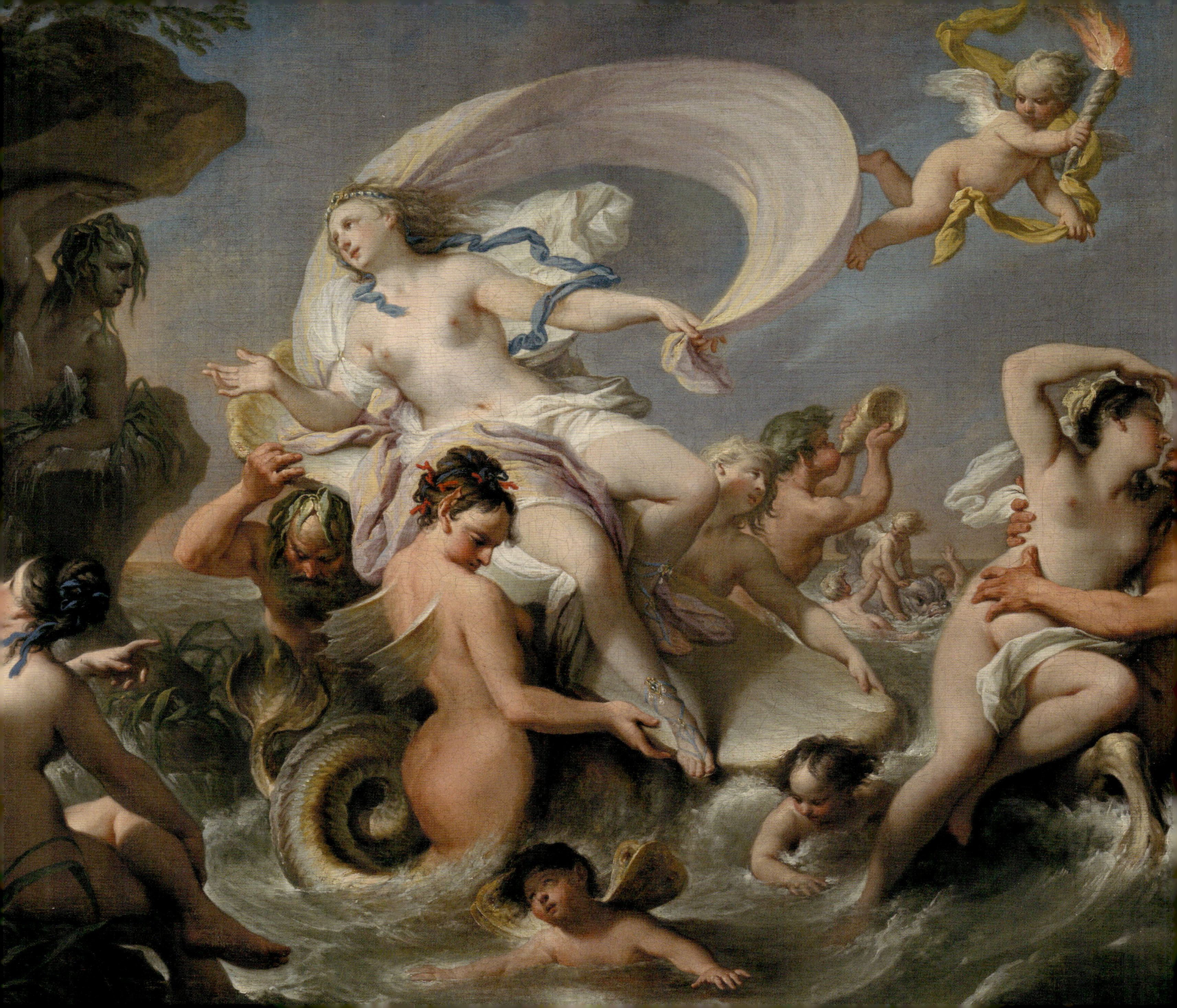

THE RISE OF IDEALISM: 18th-century art

The Triumph of Galatea,
mid-17th century
Andrea Casali

This story comes from Ovid's poem *Metamorphoses*. The sea nymph Galatea transformed her lover Acis into a river after he was killed by the fierce giant Polyphemus. The sensuous Galatea and her entourage swoop across the waves. Acis, in mid-transformation, with weedy hair and water spurting from his body, looks longingly at Galatea.

Many artists in the eighteenth century experimented with a wider variety of subjects and a lighter range of colours. This provided patrons with more choice and with works suitable for decorating their grand homes.

Many of these buyers were not Italian, but wealthy visitors undertaking the Grand Tour of Europe. Landscape views of well-known picturesque sites were popular, though these scenes were often artfully adapted by the artists. The cities and areas around Venice and Rome provided inspiration for these land and city-scapes.

A classically-based education was usual for the wealthy young men who undertook the Grand Tour, and artists also began to specialize in the depiction of subjects inspired by classical antiquity. Scenes from Greek and Roman mythology and from history provided a wealth of exciting subjects, and allegories – the use of figures to represent abstract qualities – were often a way to present moral or political messages in an attractive and visually acceptable way.

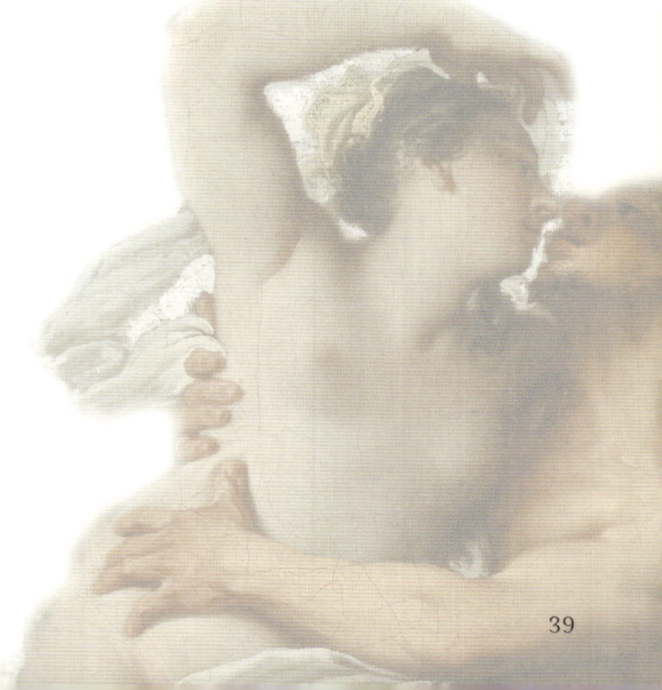

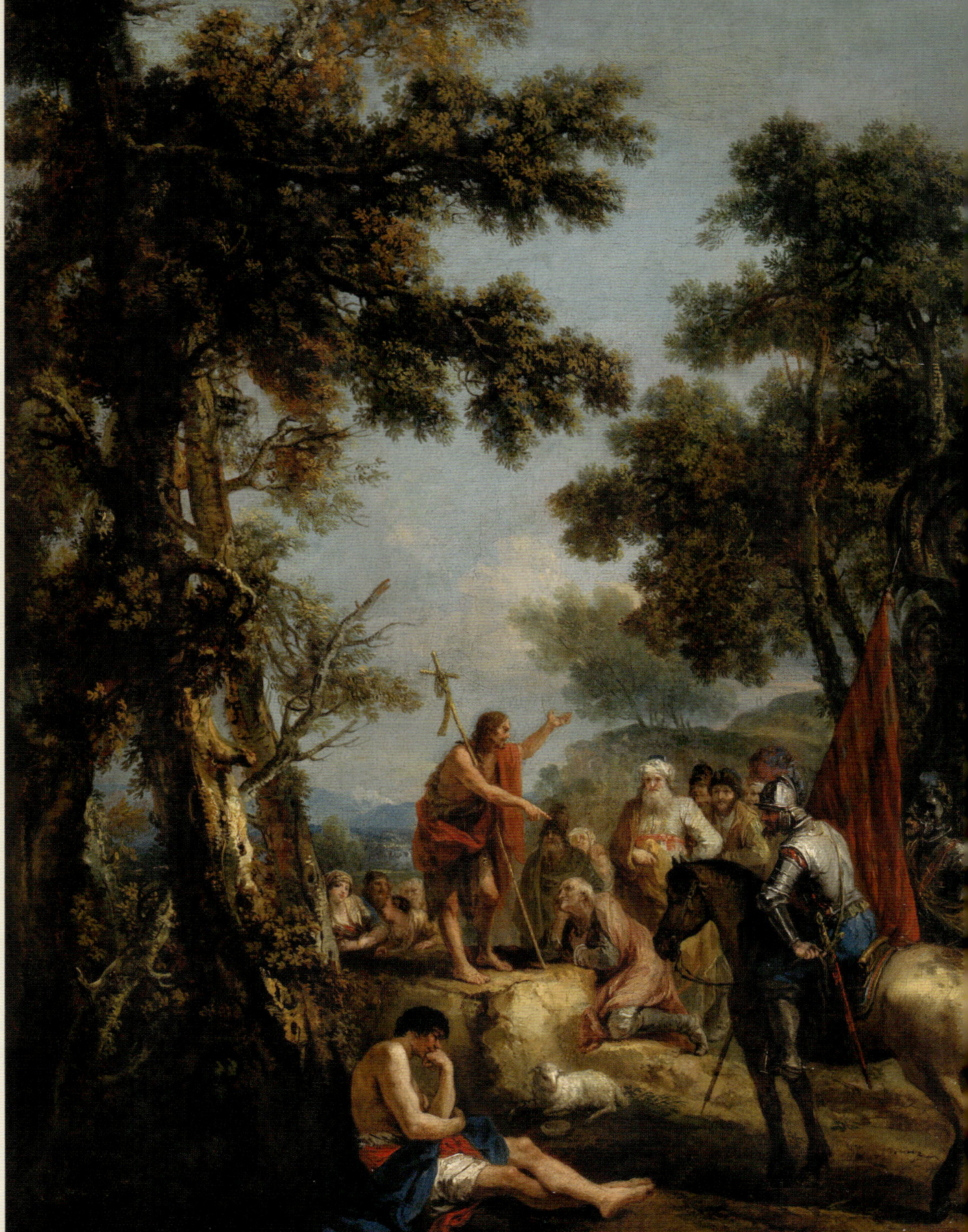

St John the Baptist Preaching,
*c.*1740–45
Francesco Zuccarelli

The Baptist's audience listens intently
in a landscape setting that frames the
group rather than overpowering it. The
pensive young man's figure is inspired by
classical sculpture, while the soldiers in
contemporary armour remind viewers that
the Baptist's message was for all time, not
just the biblical era.

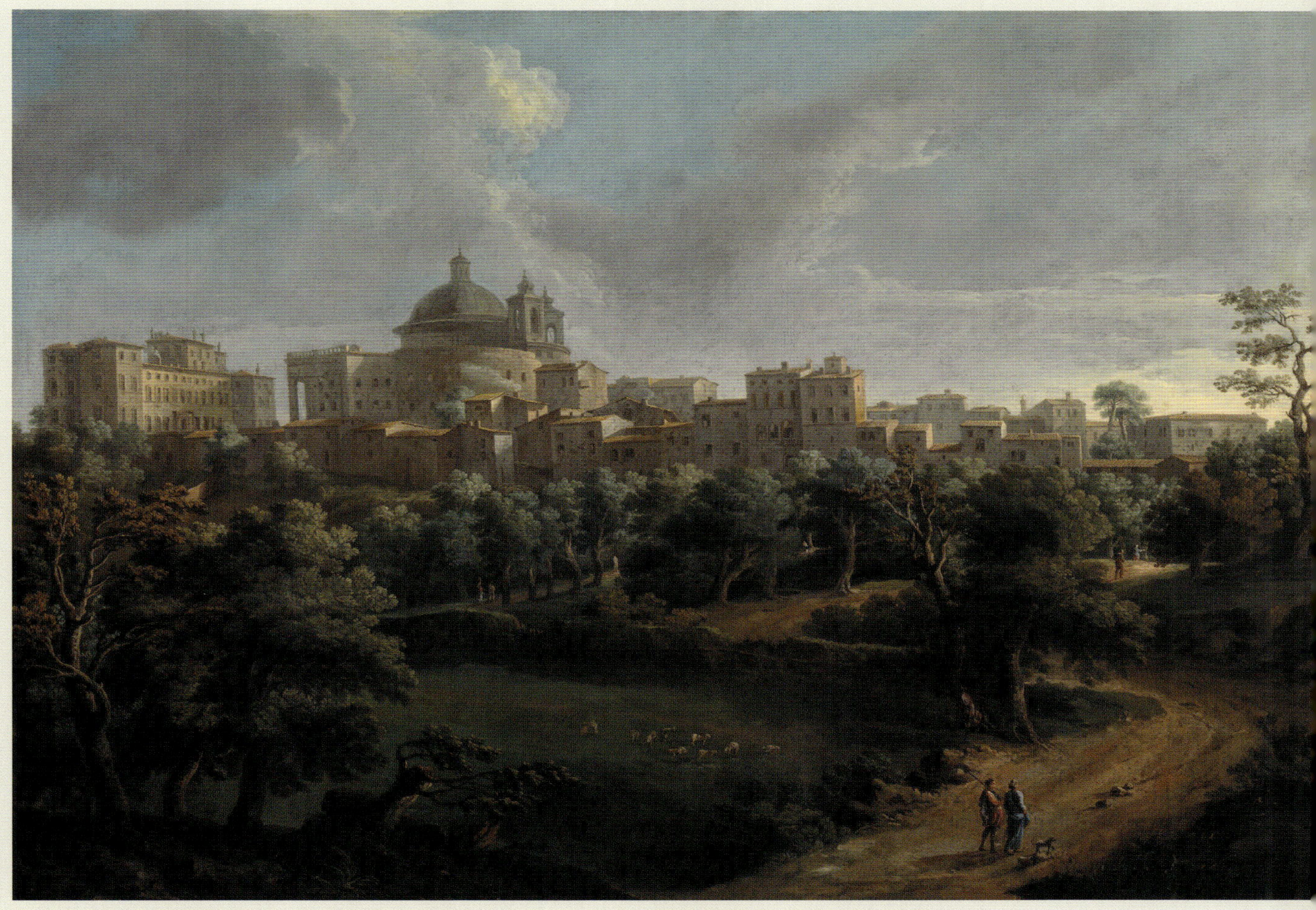

View of Ariccia, c.1760–65
Paolo Anesi

This is a view of a real town, Ariccia, near Rome, a favourite
place for Grand Tourists to visit. Such views were usually drawn
on the spot but then the artist, when working in his studio,
would add, move or delete figures and trees to give balance
and harmony to the final composition.

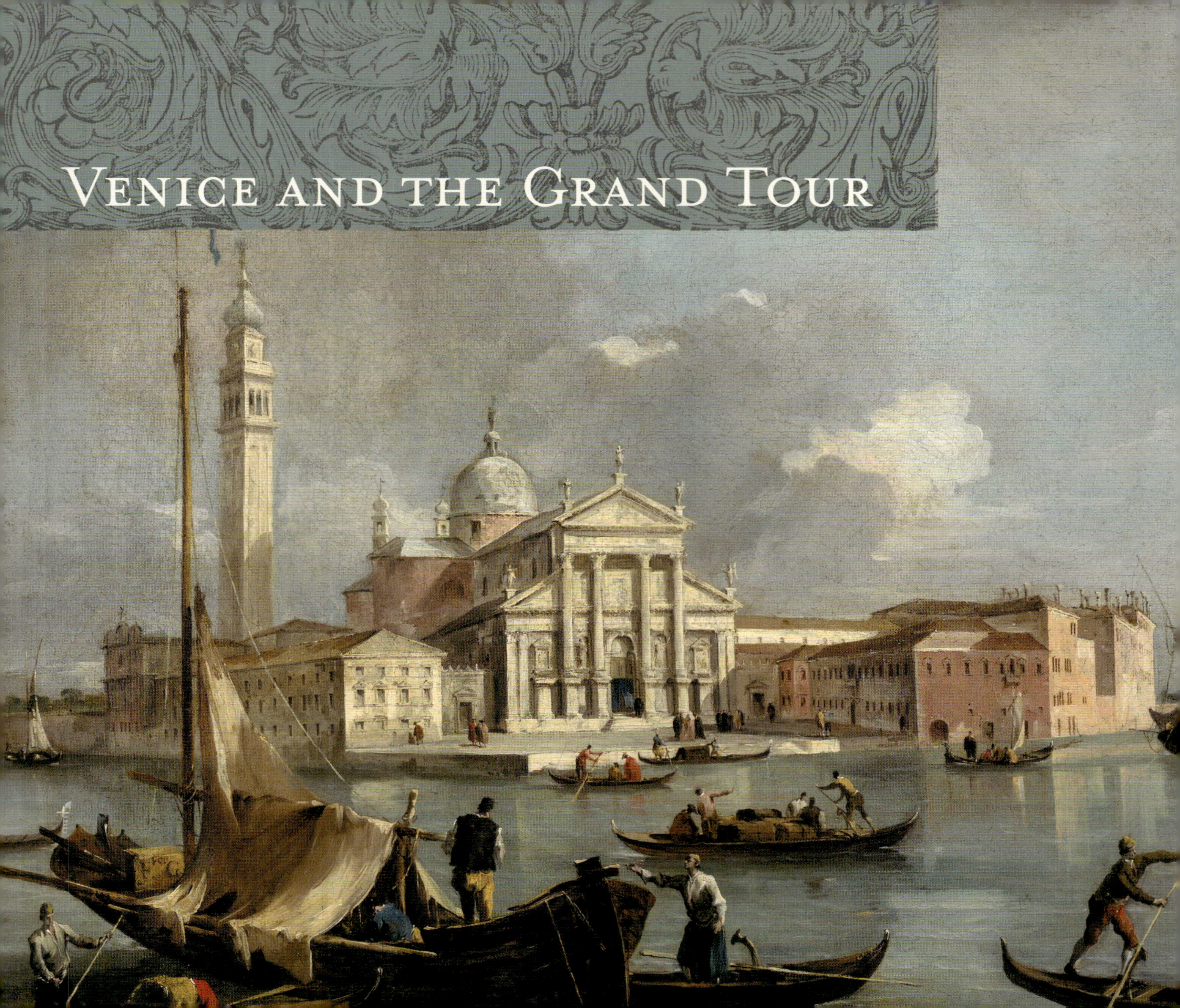

VENICE AND THE GRAND TOUR

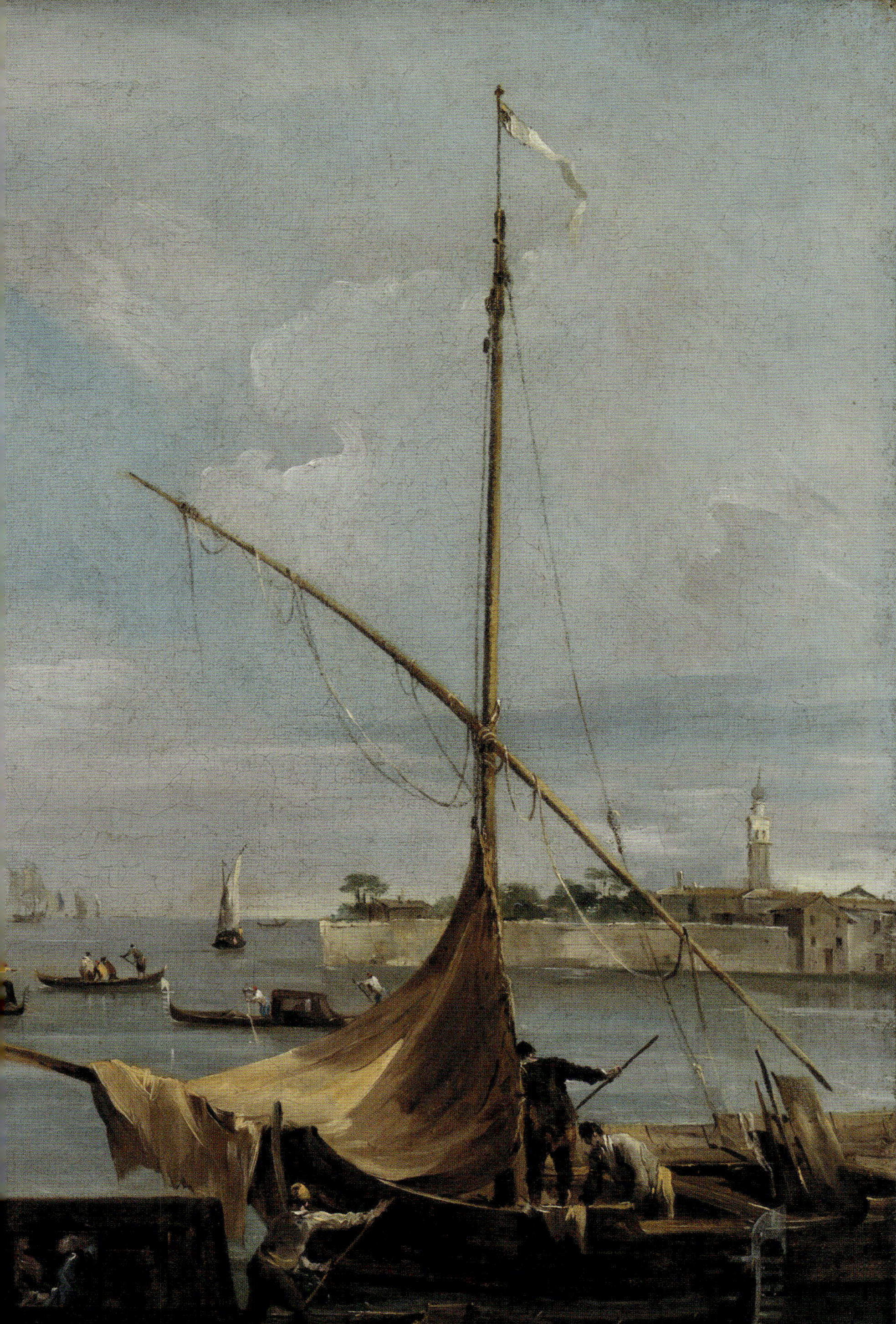

This is one of Guardi's finest views of Venice. The Church of San Giorgio Maggiore is seen from St Mark's piazzetta on the opposite side of the Grand Canal. The sky is bright but cloudy; the water of the canal is glassy; and the reflections are broken by gentle movement. Barges and gondolas with colourfully-garbed boatmen and passengers punctuate the scene.

Guardi's work is characterized by contrasting patterns of light and shade. His use of impasto – thick oil paint – emphasized, in the form of slight relief, this particular effect. Such paintings were highly sought after by wealthy British Grand Tourists, many of whom lived in country houses designed in the style of the Venetian architect Antonio Palladio.

'*Paintings … were highly sought after by wealthy Grand Tourists …*'

View of St Giorgio Maggiore,
c.1760
Francesco Guardi

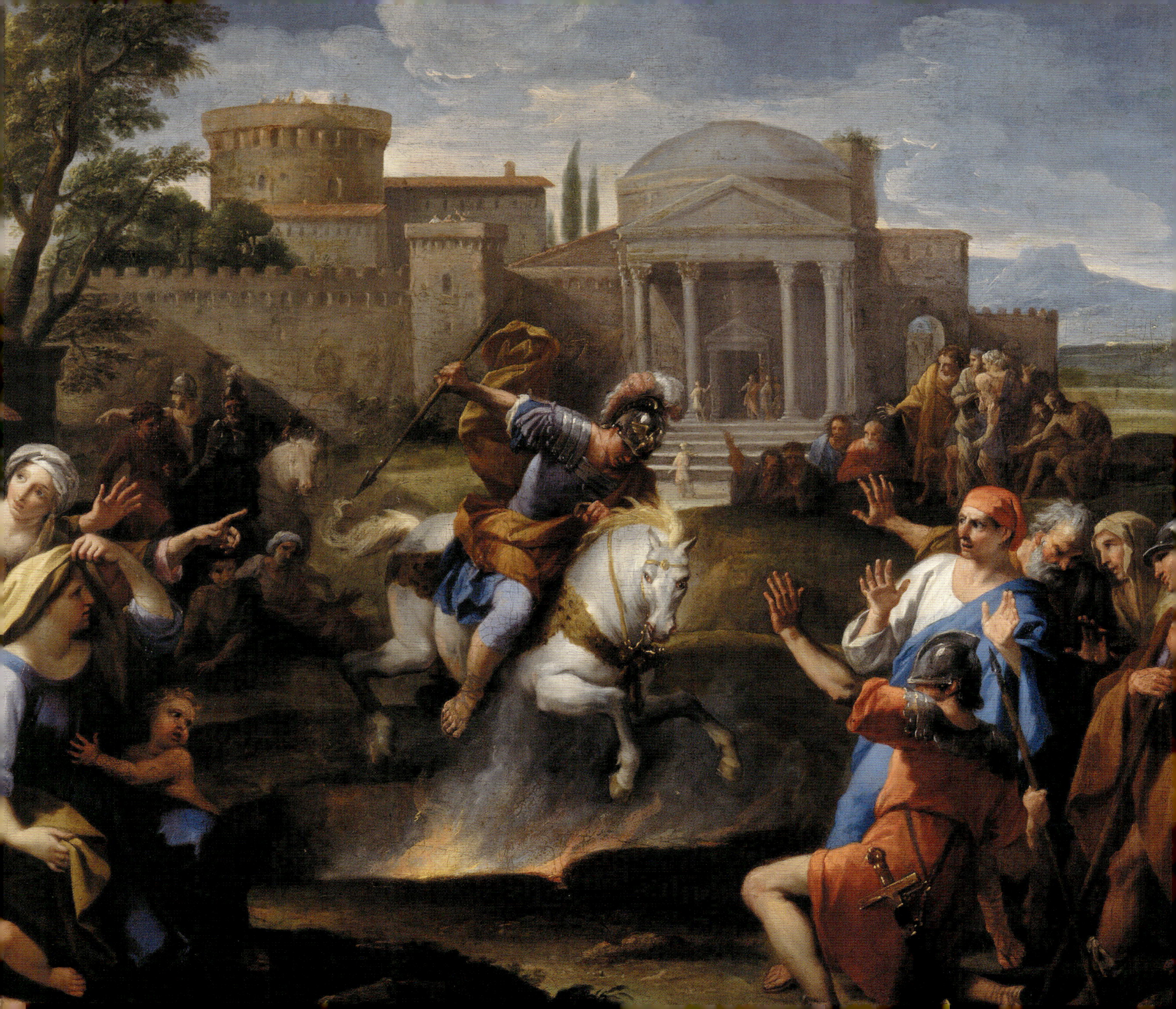

Works in Focus

The Sacrifice of Marcus Curtius, c.1715–20
Luigi Garzi

This is an example of history painting in the 'Grand Style'. These paintings often had dramatic subjects, showed a knowledge of classical literature, costume and architecture, and a carefully structured composition.

The legendary story of the Roman hero Marcus Curtius is recounted by the famous historian, Livy. A deep chasm suddenly opened up in the Roman Forum, and it was prophesied that only the sacrifice of Rome's greatest treasure could close up the dangerous opening and save the city. Marcus Curtius, a war hero, sacrificed himself by jumping, on horseback and fully armed, into the chasm, which then shut.

In the background is Garzi's version of an ancient Roman building, probably – as it is domed – based on the Pantheon, one of the most complete classical buildings to have survived in in the city.

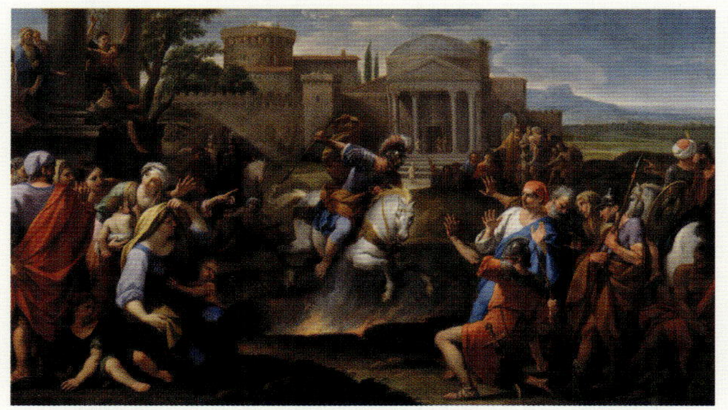

'... the epitome of most painters' scope and ambition ...'

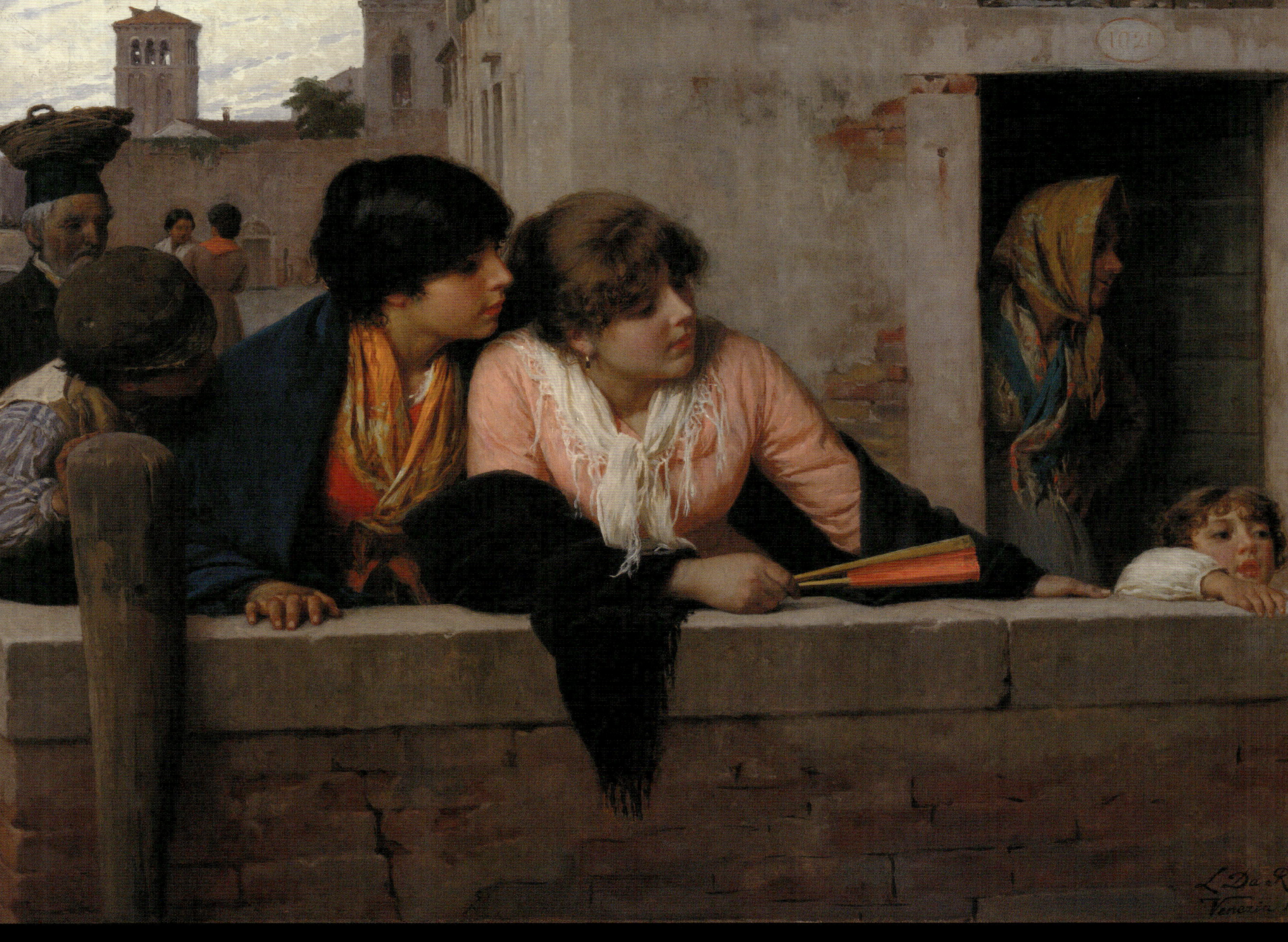

Overlooking a Canal, Venice, 1886
Luigi Da Rios

This painting depicts a scene from everyday life. Not a place on the well-trodden tourist trail, it is a back street overlooking one of the many smaller canals. The campanile in the background is that of the parish church of San Niccolò dei Mendicoli (St Nicholas of the Beggars). Lively contemporary paintings like this were popular with foreign visitors.

Early in the nineteenth century a severe form of classicism developed in both painting and sculpture. This style was particularly appropriate for depicting scenes from ancient Roman history, as seen in the work of Vincenzo Camuccini (overleaf). The artist has made an heroic attempt to depict the buildings and costume accurately.

Towards the end of the century, the modern world began to appear in popular genre scenes. Although seemingly casual and spontaneous in nature, these paintings were painstakingly composed and executed.

The exception is a meticulously-worked picture by Pietro Aldi (right) which harks back to a precise historical period – the late medieval world – and to a specific place, Siena. Some artists and craftsmen at this time were recreating the style of artefacts made by their predecessors, whose work was by now sought after by collectors all over the world.

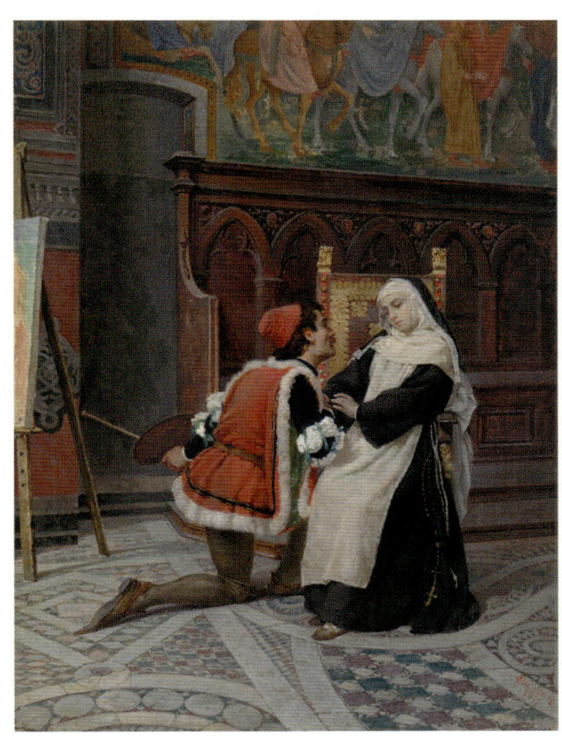

A Painter and his Model, 1879
Pietro Aldi

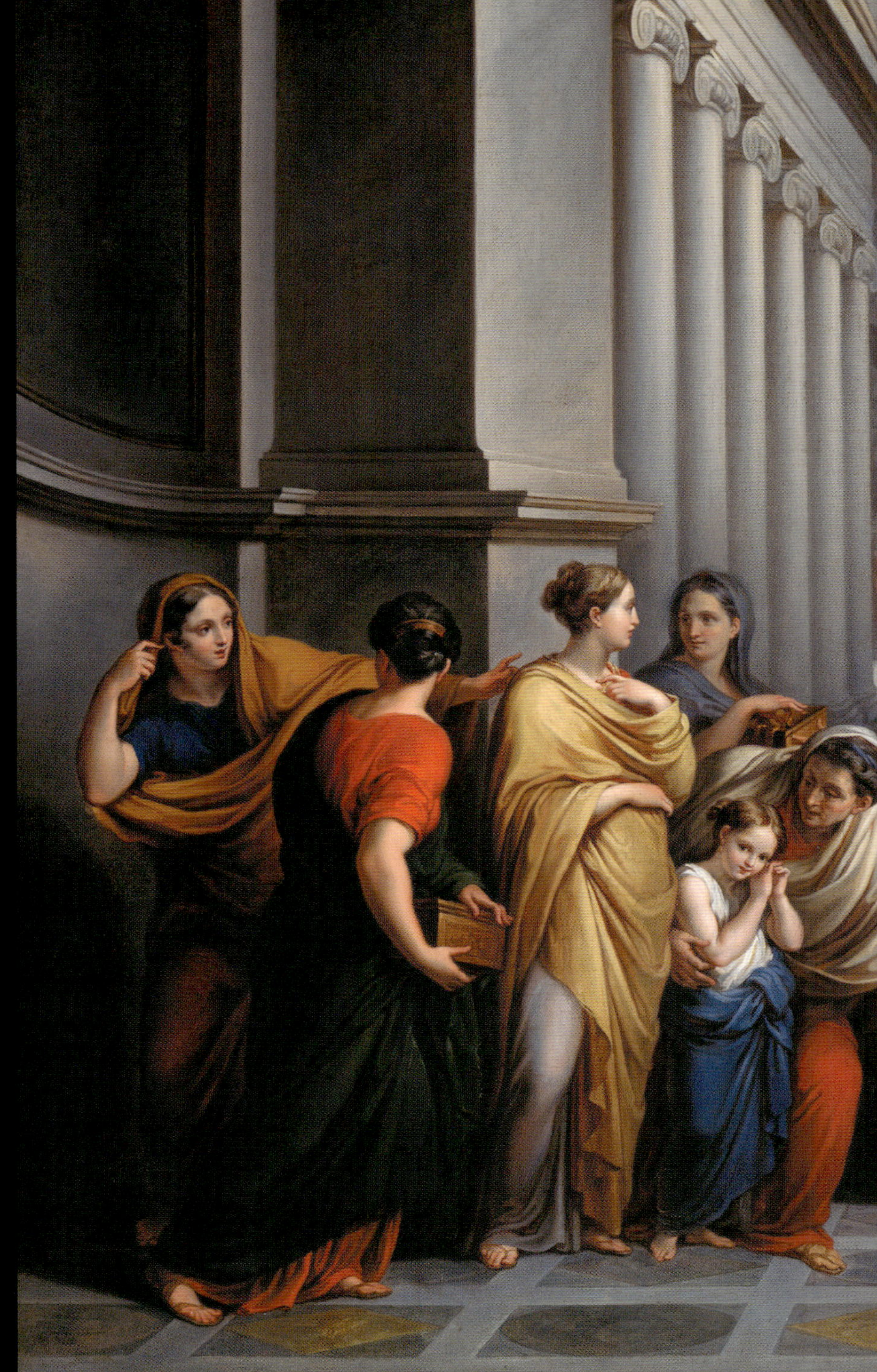

Roman Women offering their Jewellery in Defence of the State, c.1825–9
Vincenzo Camuccini

This painting is one of two commissioned from the artist in Rome by Mrs Cecilia Douglas of Orbiston, near Glasgow. It shows wealthy Roman women giving up their gold jewellery – a patriotic gesture, as the jewellery was to be melted down. The gold was used to make a bowl, sent to the shrine of Apollo at Delphi in settlement of an unfulfilled vow made by Camillus, commander of the Roman army.

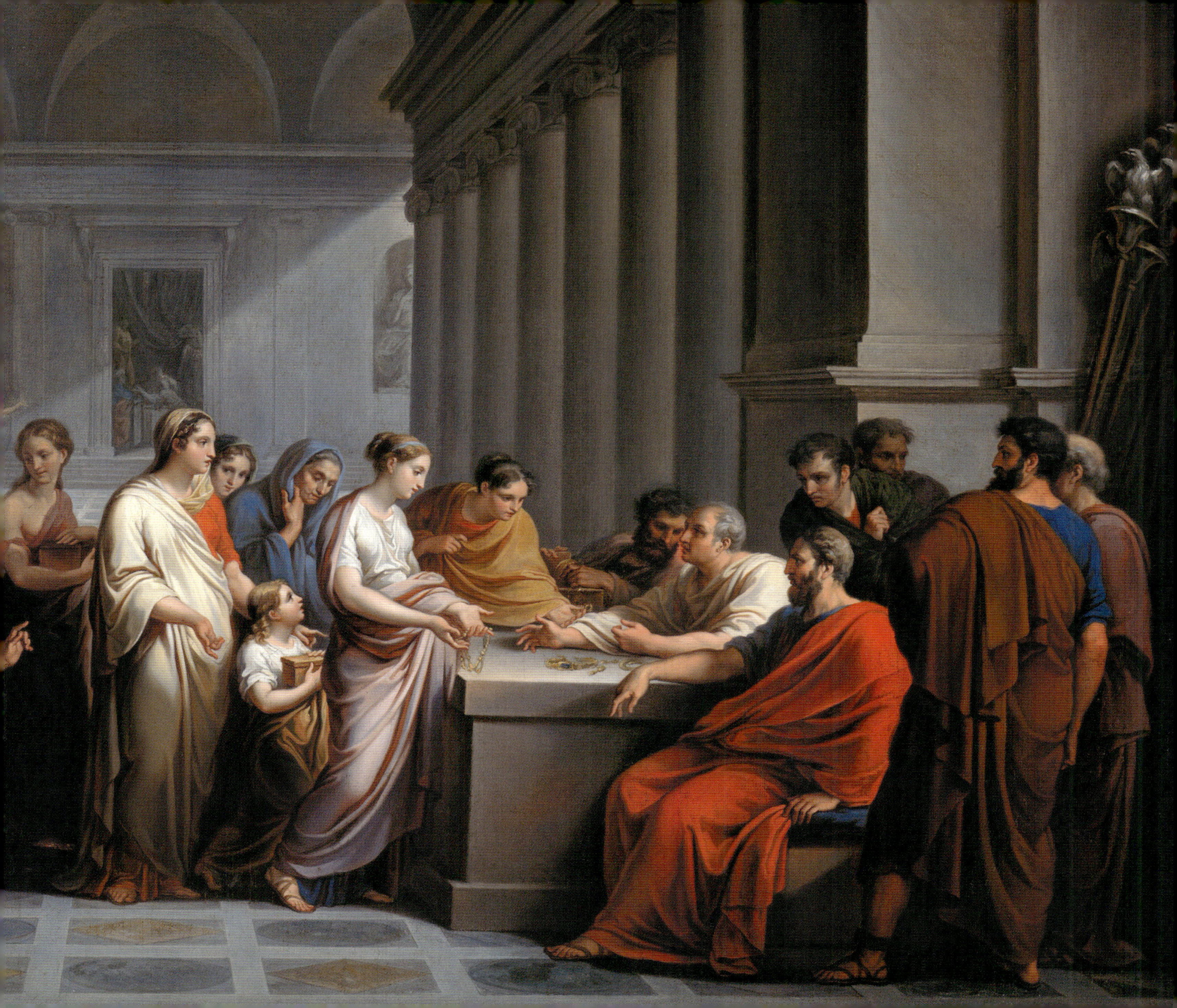

Works in Focus

This richly detailed work depicts a boy seated with an assortment of items, piled jumble-like as a still life on the table in front of him. Most of the items are oriental – dolls, a porcelain vase, and a brilliant silk robe. The velvet upholstered chair is worn, and there is a large painting on the wall behind. Is this a portrait of the boy, or is he just another element in the midst of the still life?

The Sulky Boy, 1875
Antonio Mancini

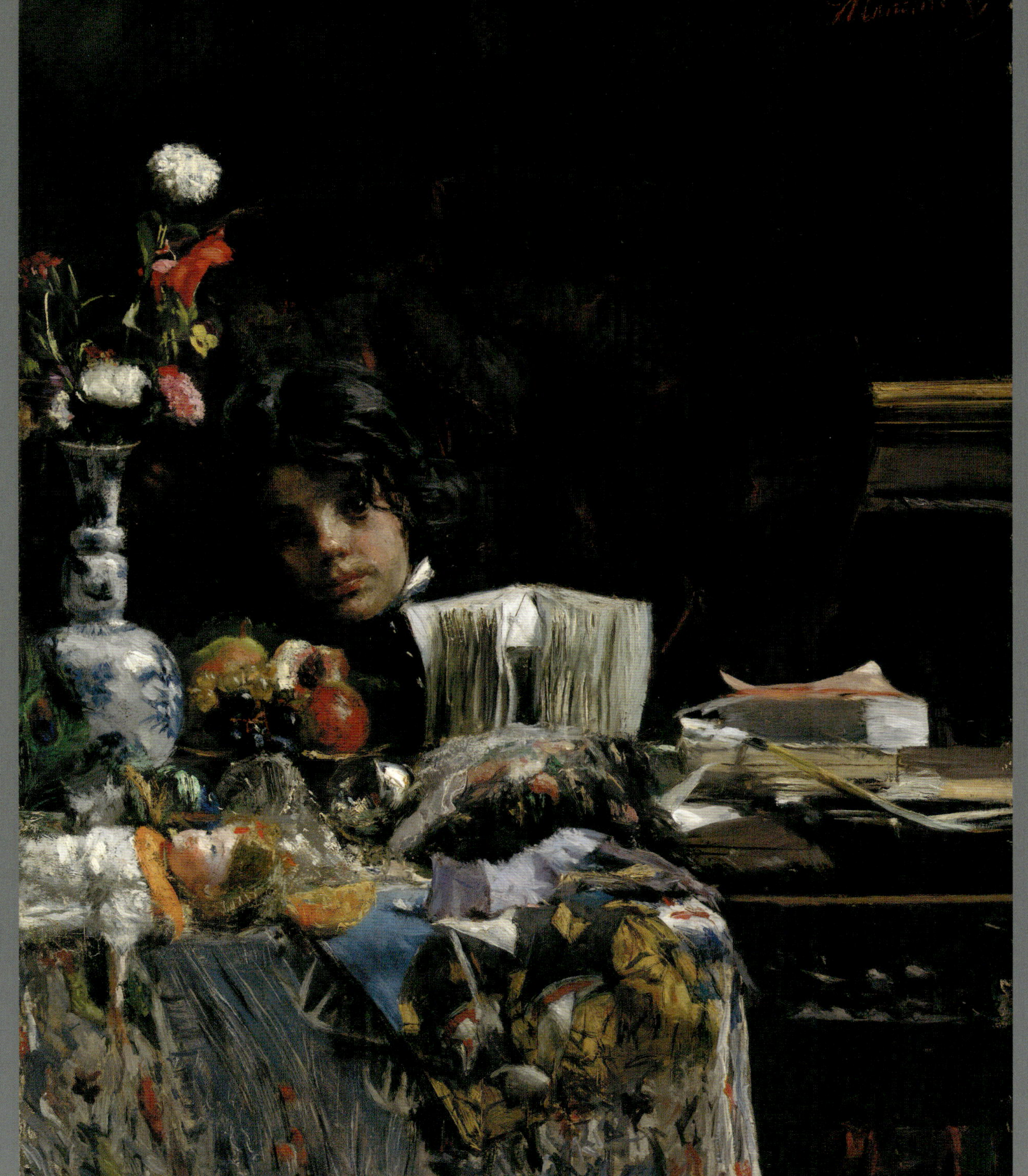

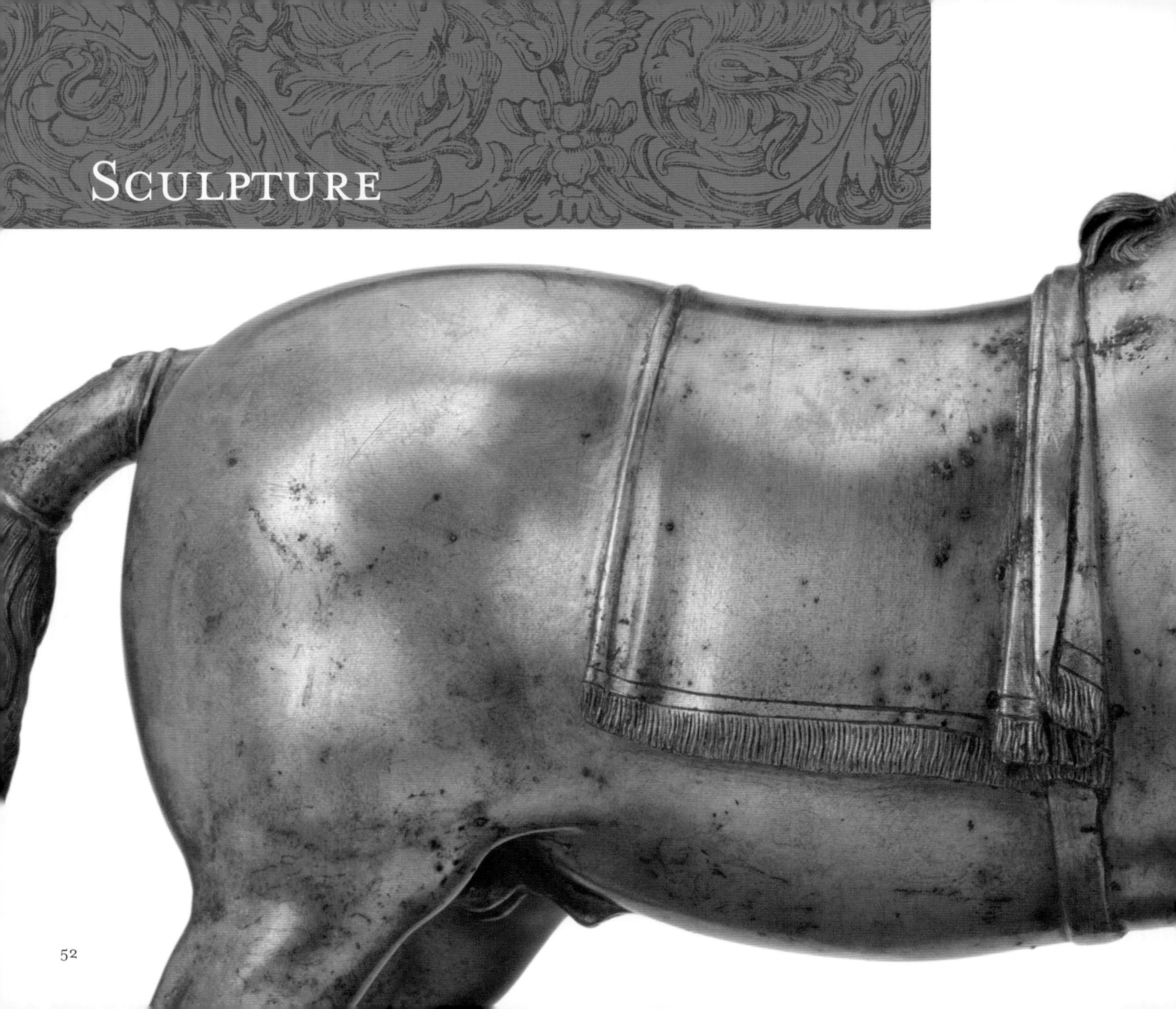

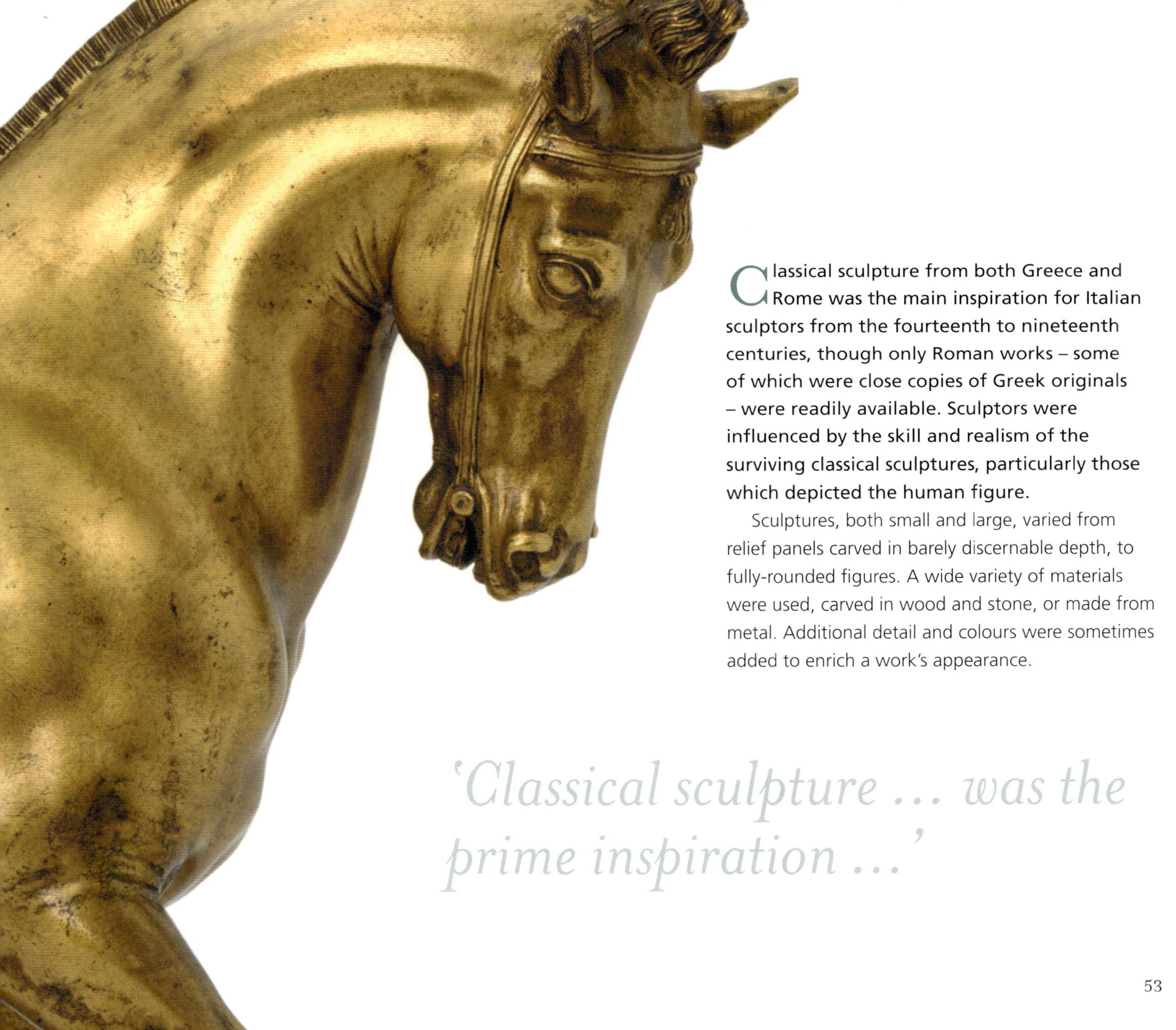

Classical sculpture from both Greece and Rome was the main inspiration for Italian sculptors from the fourteenth to nineteenth centuries, though only Roman works – some of which were close copies of Greek originals – were readily available. Sculptors were influenced by the skill and realism of the surviving classical sculptures, particularly those which depicted the human figure.

Sculptures, both small and large, varied from relief panels carved in barely discernable depth, to fully-rounded figures. A wide variety of materials were used, carved in wood and stone, or made from metal. Additional detail and colours were sometimes added to enrich a work's appearance.

'Classical sculpture … was the prime inspiration …'

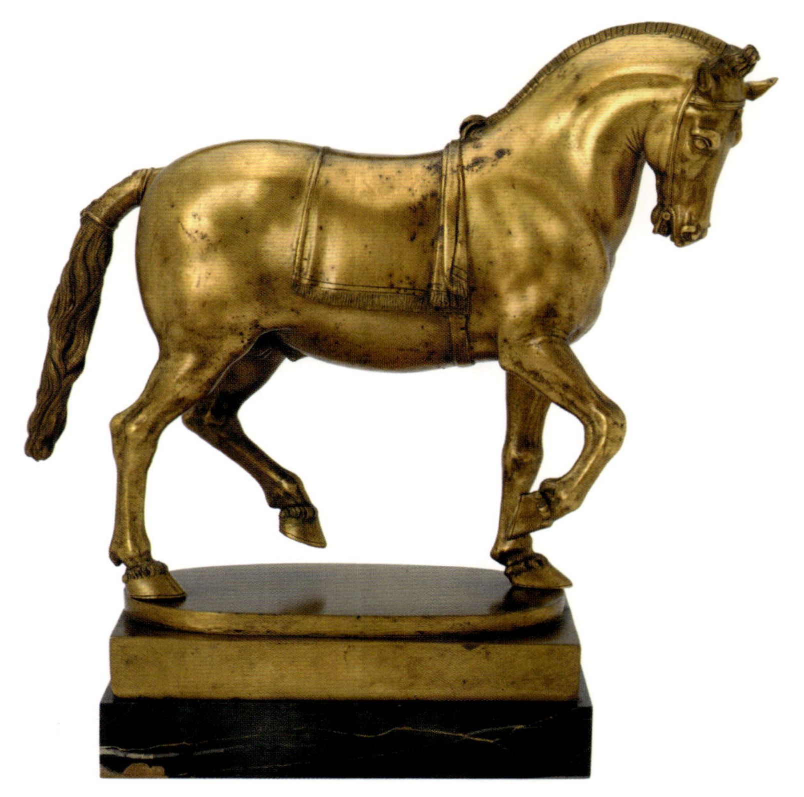

Pacing Horse, 16th century
Attributed to G.F. Susini, after Giambologna

Miniature versions of the horses used in monumental sculptures were popular subjects, particularly when made in bronze. They were often based on classical models, like the Greek horses at St Mark's Cathedral in Venice. Owners took pride in their collections of small bronzes, admiring the quality of the craftsmanship. Many of these sculptures were enhanced by gilding.

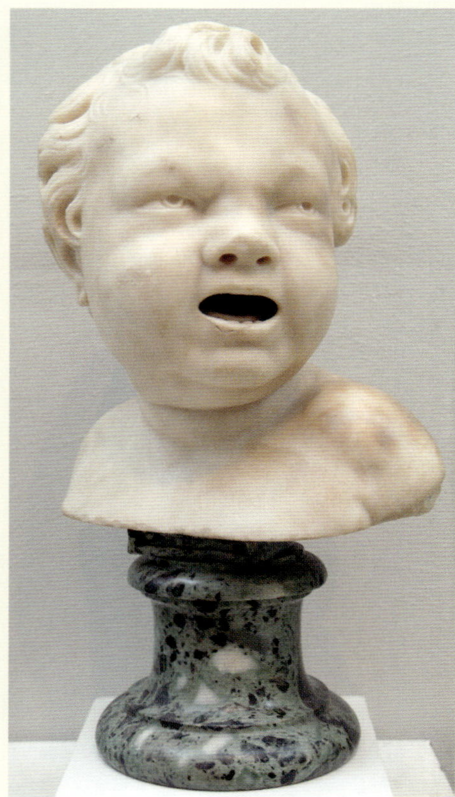

Head of a Boy, c.1480
Benedetto da Maiano

This charming marble head, made in Florence around 1480, is in the antique style favoured by most Renaissance sculptors. Chubby young children ('*putti*' in Italian) appear in both religious and secular art, and are often very lifelike.

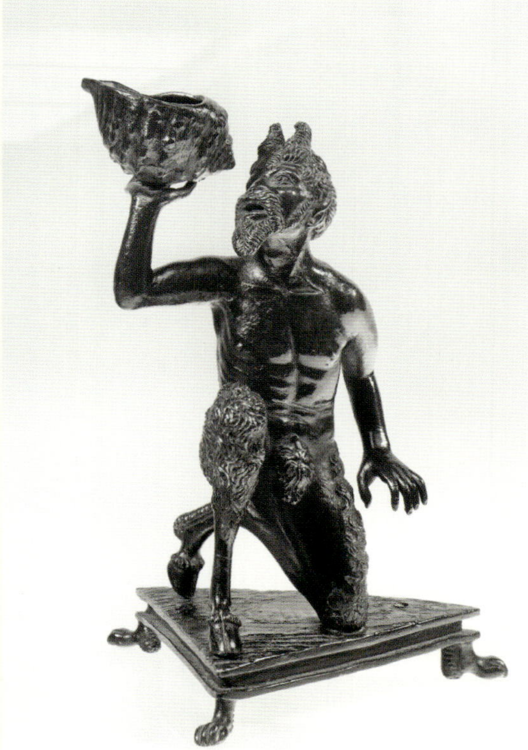

**Inkwell in the Form of a Satyr Holding a Shell,
late 15th or early 16th-century
Calzetta Severo**

Bronze sculptures were much admired during the
Renaissance. Sculptures, incorporating satyrs –
creatures from classical myth, half-man and half-goat
– holding shells as ink containers, were popular. The
mix of fine art and humour remains as engaging
today as it was when first used.

Works in Focus

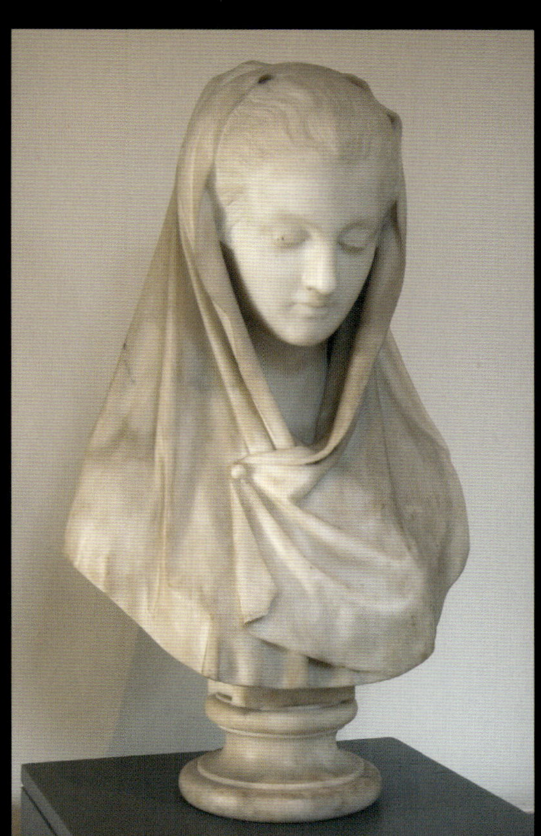

Modesty, mid-late 19th century
Giosuè Argenti, Italy

Modesty is one of Argenti's most
significant works. The young lady
gently bows her head, her eyes
downcast and submissive. A quiet
smile plays on her lips.

The Arts of War and Defence

**Rapier, c.1580,
Frederic Picinino**

**Parrying Dagger
16th century,
unknown maker**

Finely-crafted swords and daggers were made to be used by civilians. Often they had beautifully decorated hilts (handles), with sweeping bars to help protect the users' hands, as on this rapier. Its chiselled decoration is classical in style, featuring horsemen in combat and medallion portrait heads. Rapiers were often used with companion weapons like this dagger, which would be held in the left hand.

The design and manufacture of body-protective armour and weapons is now viewed as a purely commercial venture; they are products. This was also the case in the medieval and Renaissance periods, but at that time their designers and makers were classed as artists on a par with painters and sculptors. Plate armour was made to measure; by its very nature it needed to fit its owner perfectly, literally from head to toe.

But both armour and weapons were also subject to whims of fashion; styles and decoration changed from year to year, and owners could request certain details to meet their personal preferences – perhaps an image, emblem or inscription relating to the dangerous, even deadly, nature of its use. The high cost of commissioning such armour or weaponry ensured fine pieces were viewed as status symbols for the élite of the knightly classes.

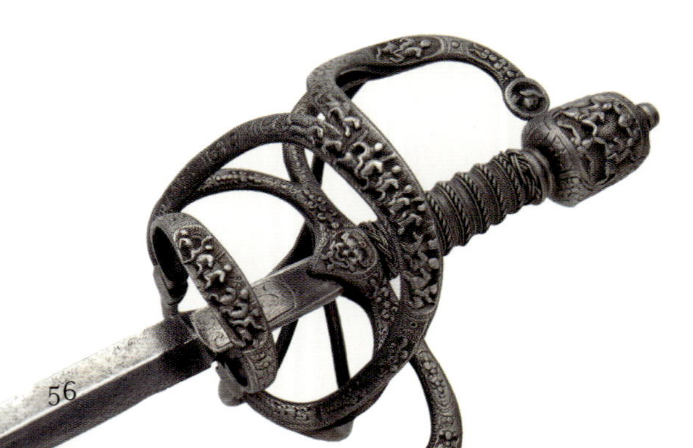

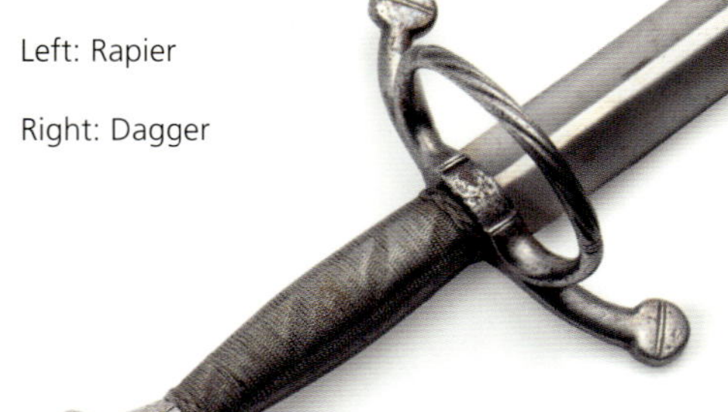

Left: Rapier

Right: Dagger

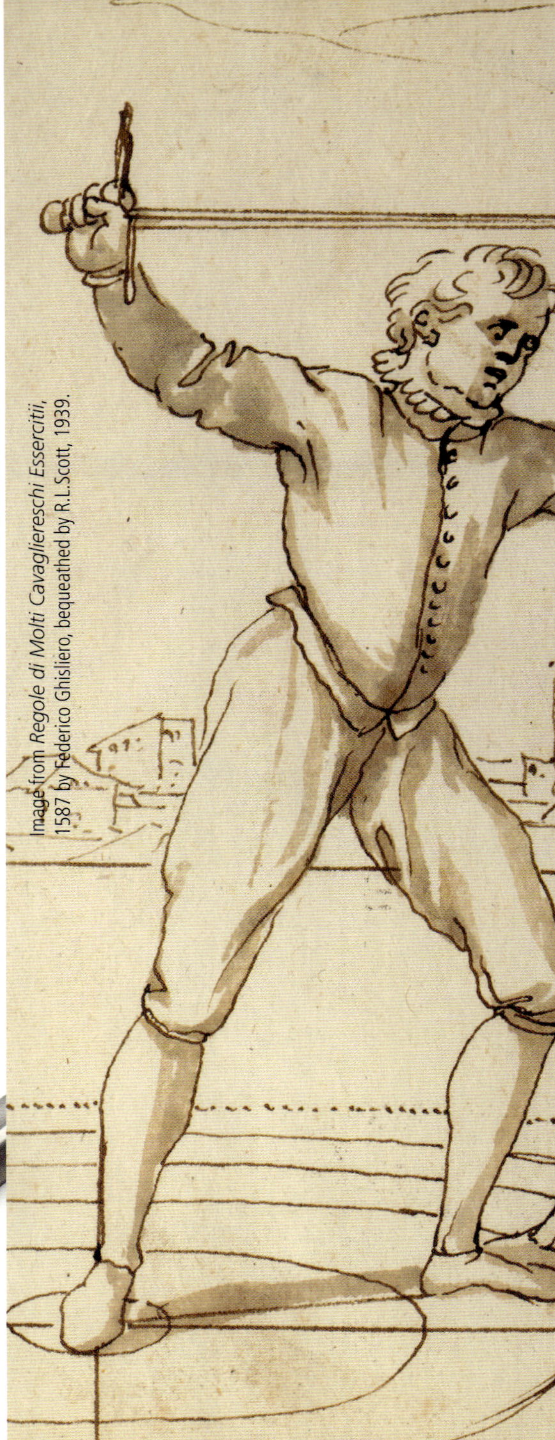

Image from *Regole di Molti Cavagliereschi Essercitii*, 1587 by Federico Ghisliero, bequeathed by R.L.Scott, 1939.

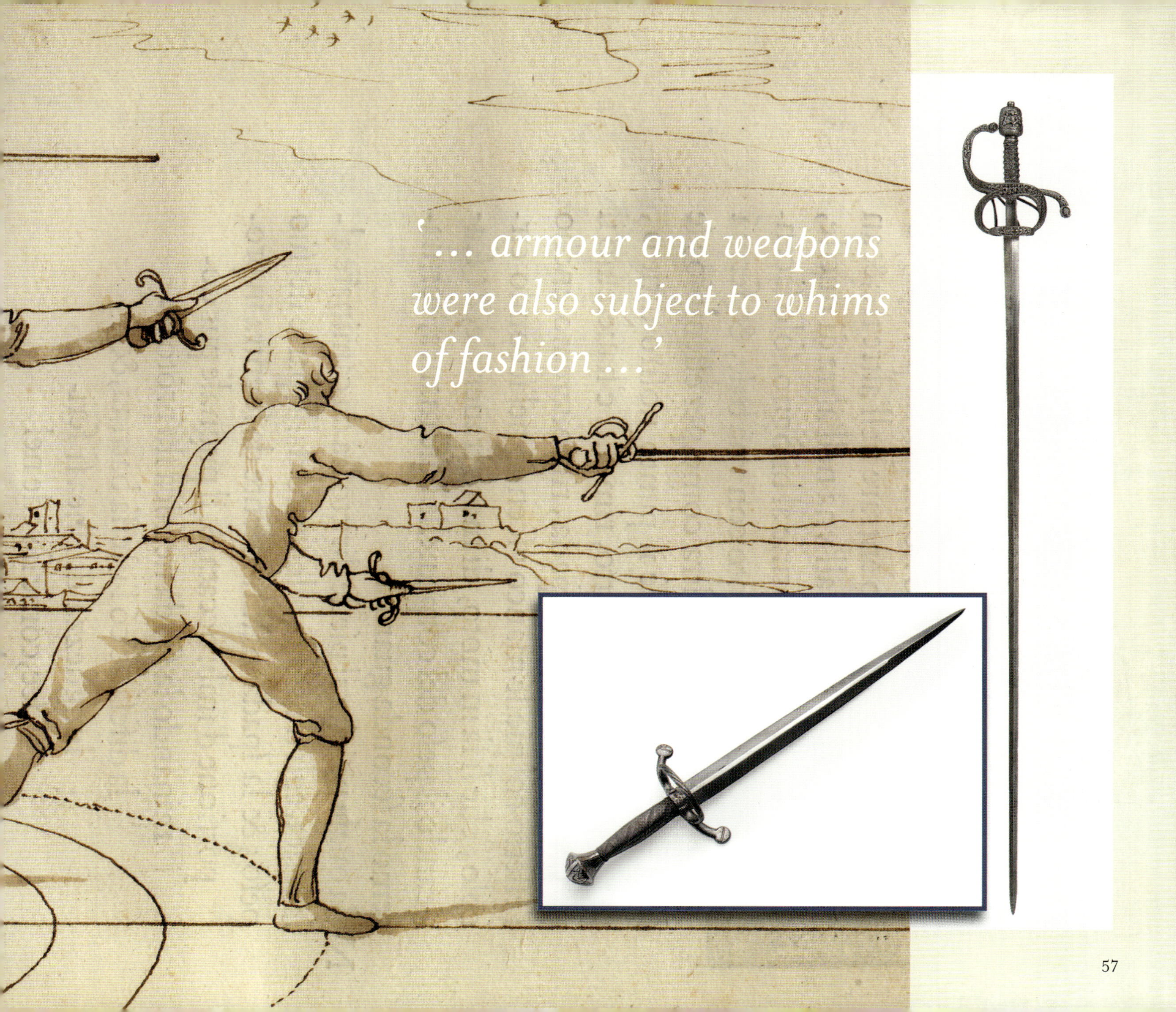

'… armour and weapons
were also subject to whims
of fashion …'

The 'Avant Armour', *c.*1440
Corio Workshop, Milan

Men of wealth and status across Europe aspired to own a fine harness (complete armour) made in Milan. This city's craftsmen were renowned for their skill in the manufacture of armour of tempered steel. AVANT – meaning 'forward!' – is engraved on the breastplate and gives the armour its name. Other inscriptions ask God, the Virgin Mary and Jesus to protect the wearer.

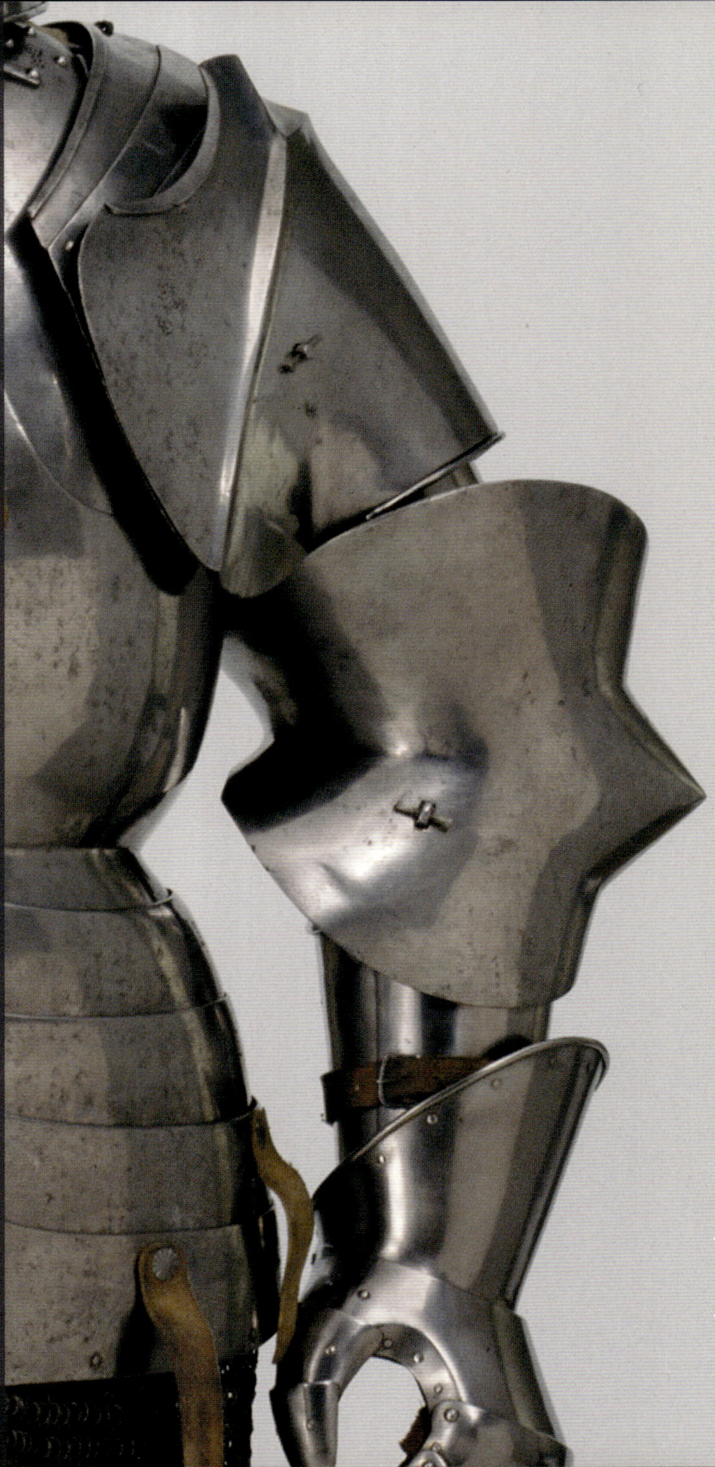

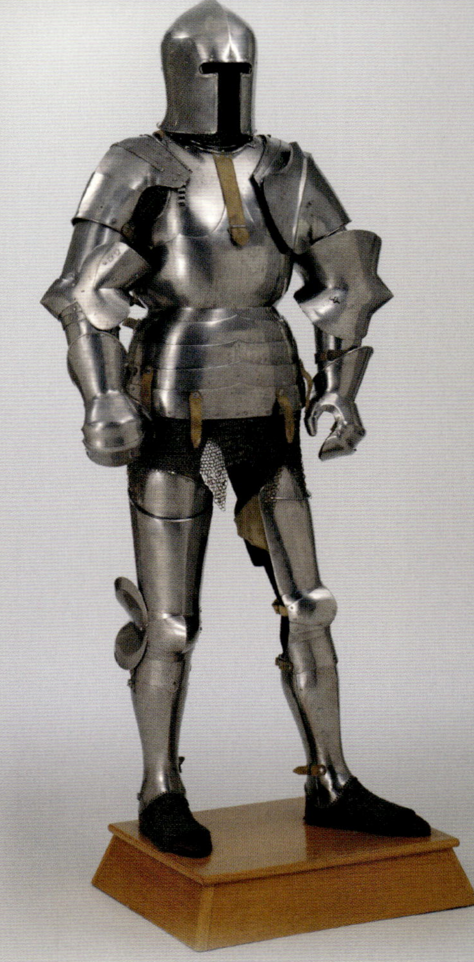

'This city's craftsmen were renowned for their skill …'

Works in Focus

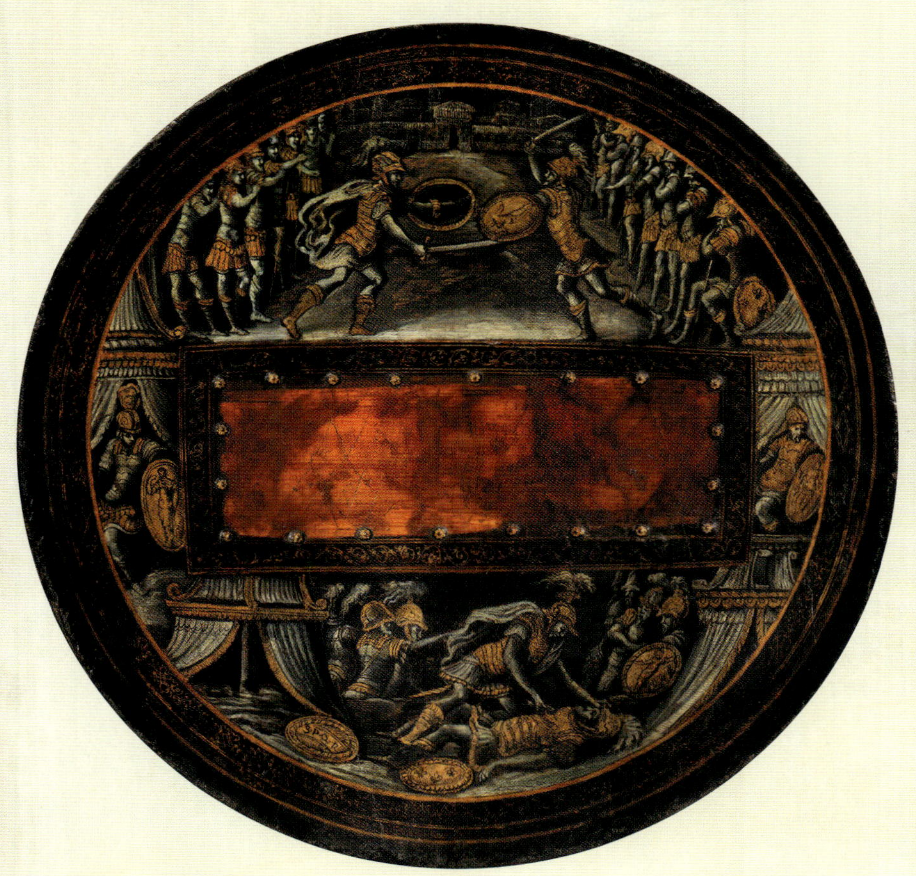

Pageant shield, Italy,
mid-16th century

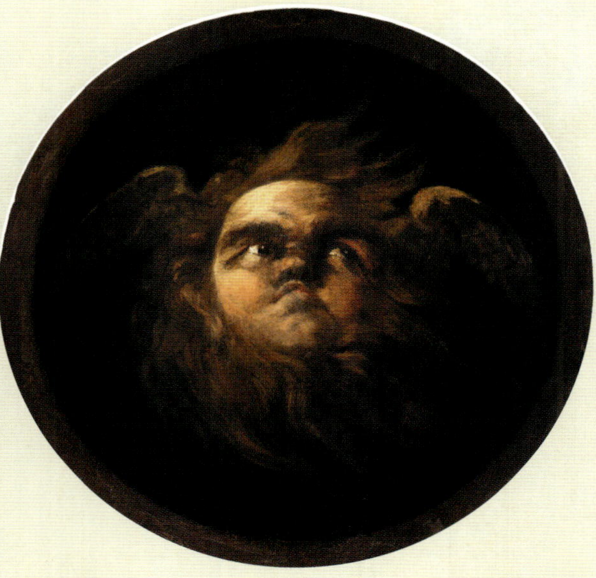

Elaborately-decorated pageant shields were carried in processions. Totally impractical, they were made in much the same way as paintings. This one has a monster's head which brings to mind the mythical Medusa, who turned all who looked at her to stone. The reverse, showing a Roman battle would not have been visible to others.

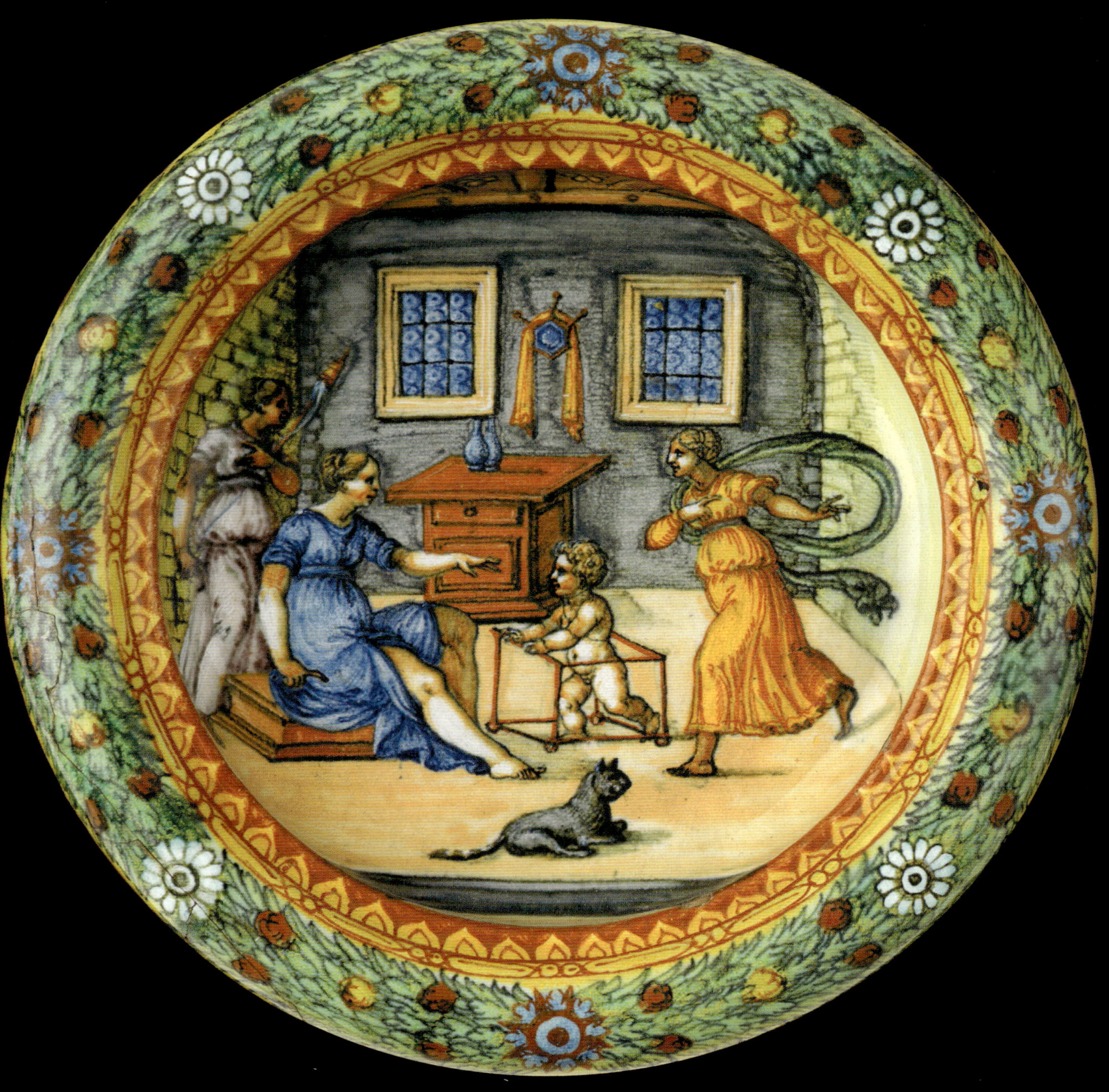

Dish from a Birthing Set, c.1525

This dish, made in Urbino around 1525, gives a fascinating insight into a 'typical' Renaissance interior. It originally formed part of a set of ceramic vessels given to a new mother for use during her lying-in period. The domestic details of the baby-walker and cat are particularly charming, while the garland of laurel on the rim underlines the celebratory function of such a gift.

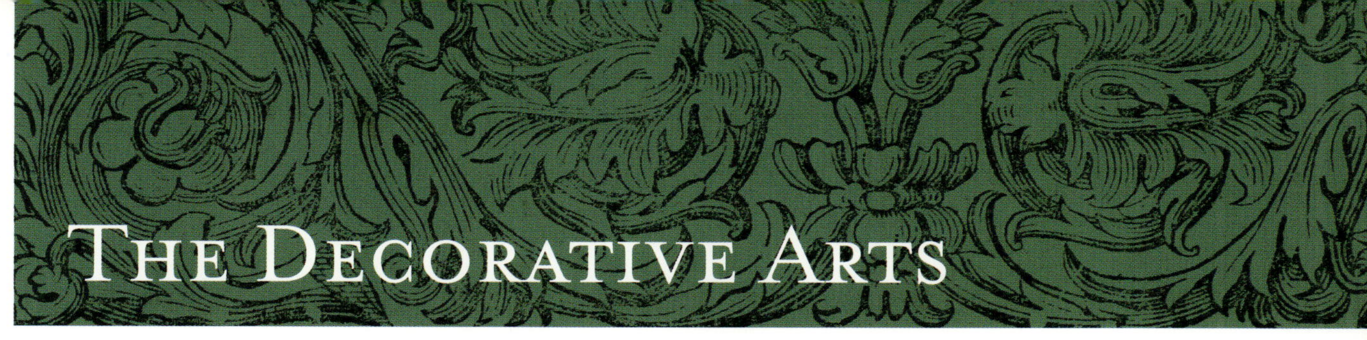

THE DECORATIVE ARTS

Decorative arts (sometimes called applied arts), include ceramics, glass, textiles and metalwork. In medieval and early Renaissance Italy skilled artisans were viewed as equally important as painters and sculptors. Their work was exported all over the known world, and purchased by royalty.

Nonetheless the making of ceramics, glass and jewellery, however fine, began to be regarded as much less prestigious. These makers' skills were eventually integrated into the manufacturing industry. Even when they revived and used traditional materials and methods, and their high-quality products were limited to a specialized field of production, these makers never achieved the renown of their historical predecessors. It is only relatively recently that these skills have been more fully appreciated, and the artefacts admired accordingly.

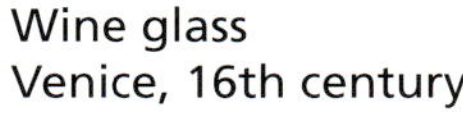

**Wine glass
Venice, 16th century**

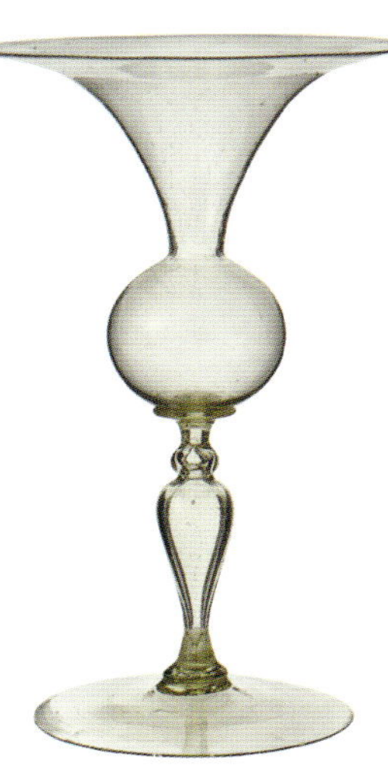

This fine glass is of a type described as '*cristallo*' or 'crystal'. Venetian glass did not contain lead, as modern crystal glass does, and it was difficult to remove all impurities from the raw materials, leaving the finished piece as colourless as possible. This delicately flaring wine glass is feather-light, making its survival all the more miraculous.

**Enamelled Dish
Venice, late 15th century**

This luxurious dish may have been used for rinsing diners' fingers during meals. The glossy jewel-like effect of the enamels is enhanced by delicate detailing in gold leaf. The central disk shows a sprig of laurel and a Latin motto '*UT LAURUS VIRTUS*' ('Virtue comes from the laurel tree').

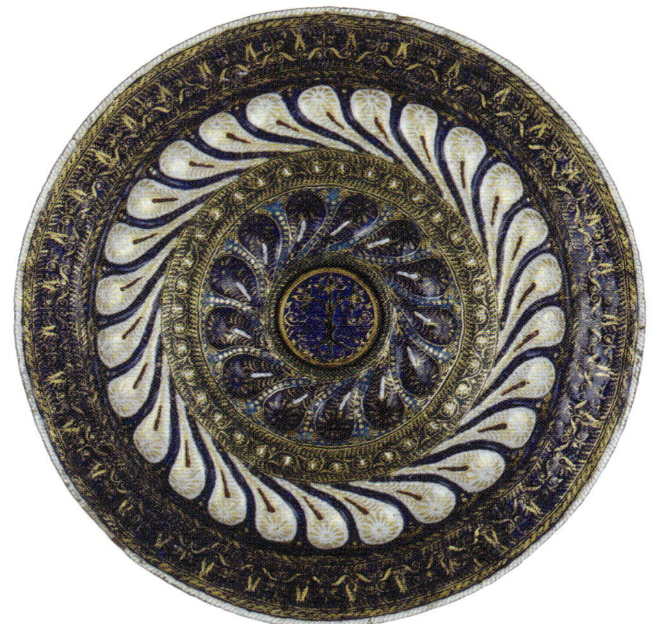

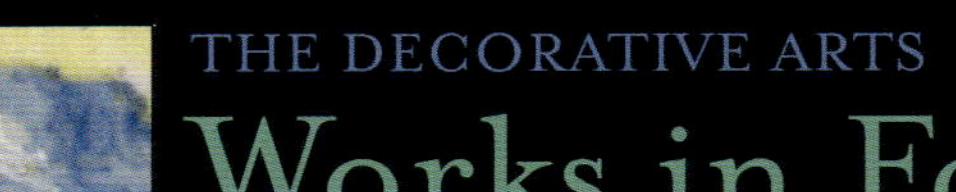

Works in Focus

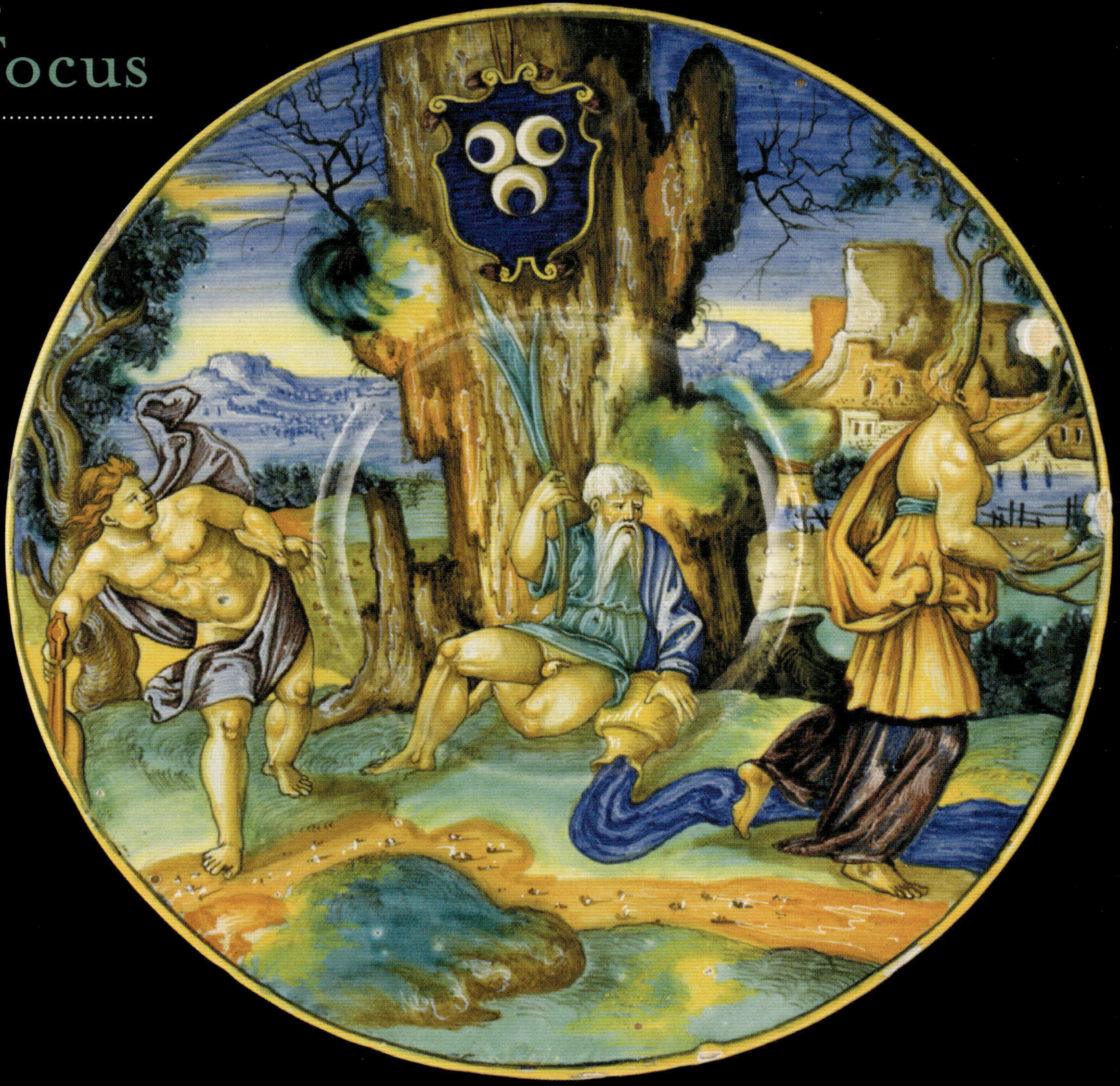

Plate with Apollo and Daphne, *c.*1530
Francesco Xanto Avelli,
Urbino

This plate illustrates an episode
from the Roman poet Ovid's
Metamorphoses. It shows the
story of the Greek god Apollo,
who fell madly in love with the
nymph Daphne, and chased
her in order to seduce her.
Here she calls for help from
her father, a river god (in the
centre), who changes her into
a laurel tree. The inscription on
the reverse reads 'Apollo, who
chases and loves his Daphne.
Fable and history'.

Francesco Xanto Avelli

Francesco Xanto Avelli was one of the most prolific pottery painters working during the Renaissance period. He worked in the complex technique known as maiolica. Designs were painted directly on to an absorbent glaze layer on a blank pot. It was then fired in a kiln, where the extreme heat fixed the coloured designs permanently. Xanto signed most of his work, and often added other information on the reverse – dates, information on his literary sources, and even extracts from his own poems.

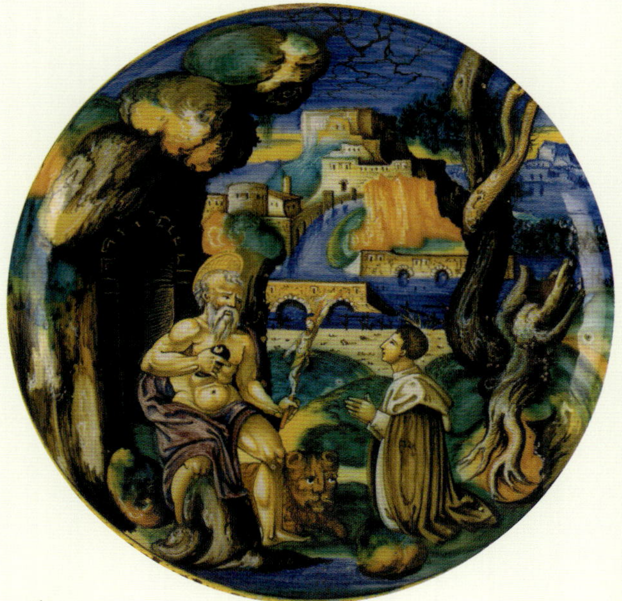

Above:
Plate with St Jerome and the Beato Colombini,
*c.*1528–30
Francesco Xanto Avelli, Urbino

This plate shows the Blessed Giovanni Colombini, a Sienese penitent who died in 1367. He founded a religious order, the Apostolic Clerics of St Jerome. He kneels before St Jerome, who sits beside his attribute of a lion.

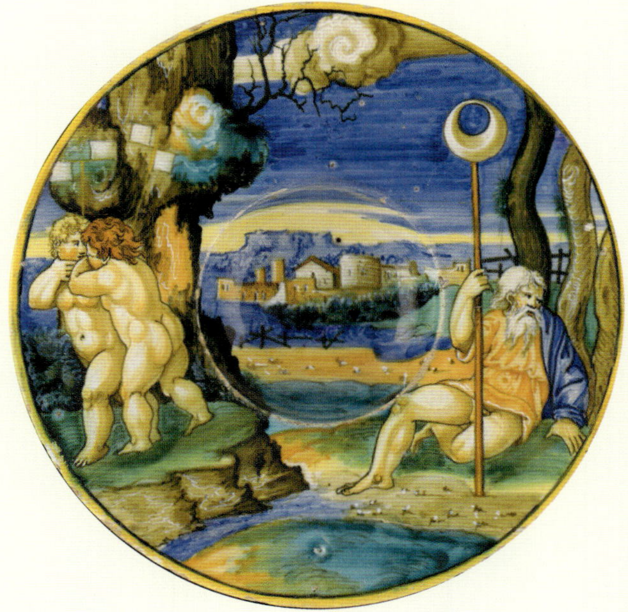

Left:
Plate with an Allegorical Scene, *c.*1528–30
Francesco Xanto Avelli, Urbino

Two small boys, carrying toy windmills, whisper to each other – probably laughing at the old man sitting nearby. The inscription on the reverse '*Tich, Tach, Nota*', perhaps translates as 'Tick, Tock, Take note.' This is a reference to the passing of time and the fact that everyone inevitably becomes old. The symbol on the man's pole, which resembles a clock's pendulum, is very like the armorial symbols on the 'Apollo and Daphne' plate, so these two pieces could come from the same service.

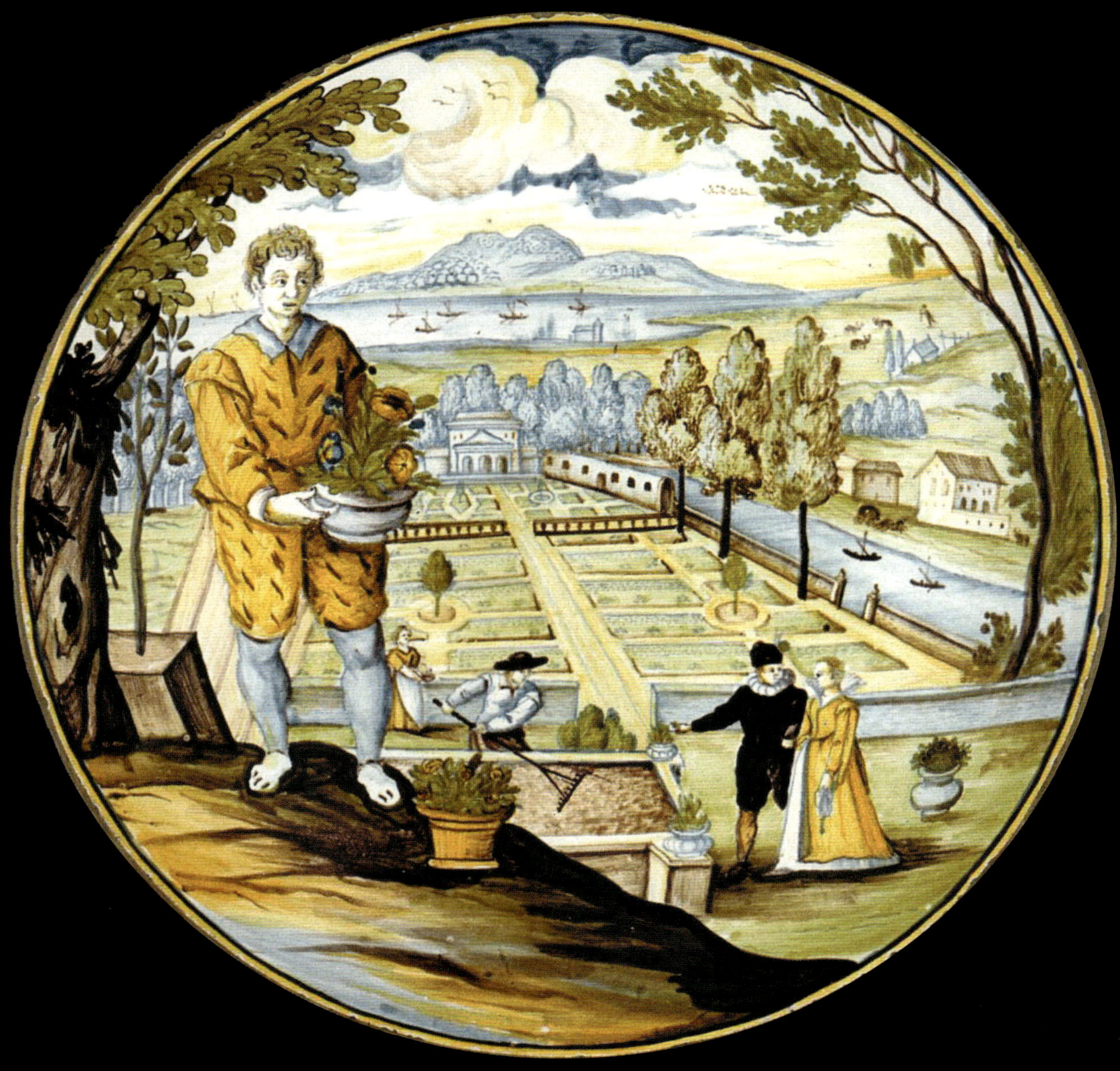

Dish with Garden Scene, 1655–1723
Carlo Antonio Grue

The Grue family were prolific producers of maiolica in Castelli. This plate shows a wonderful view of a contemporary formal garden. A man stands on a hill holding a plant pot while an assistant rakes a bed below. The owner of the garden indicates points of interest to his female companion.

Anne Hull Grundy

Mrs Anne Hull Grundy was a notable collector of antique and modern jewellery. In 1976 she gave over 900 pieces to Glasgow Museums. These included jewellery from European countries as well as British-made items. These examples are typical of the kind of souvenirs which would have been brought home by visitors, either to wear or as gifts – they are fine and beautifully made.

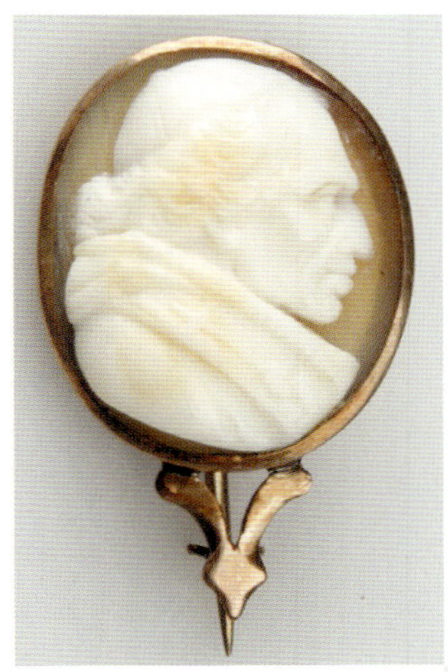

Above:
Brooch with Cameo Portrait of Pope Pius VII, 19th century

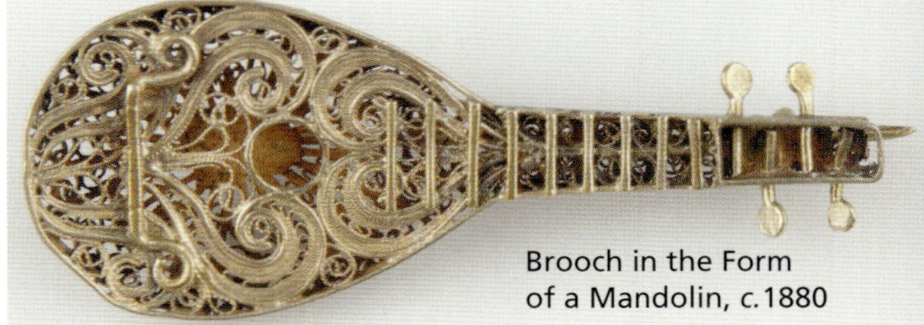

Brooch in the Form of a Mandolin, *c.*1880

Mrs Hull Grundy gave over 900 pieces to Glasgow Museums

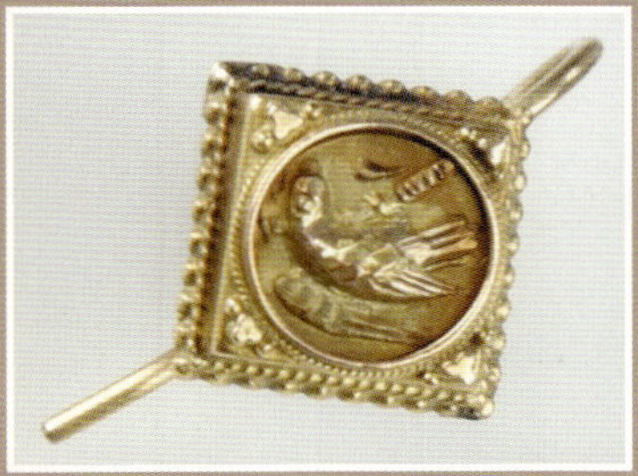

Right:
One of a Pair of Earrings, 19th century in the style of Fortunato Pio Castellani

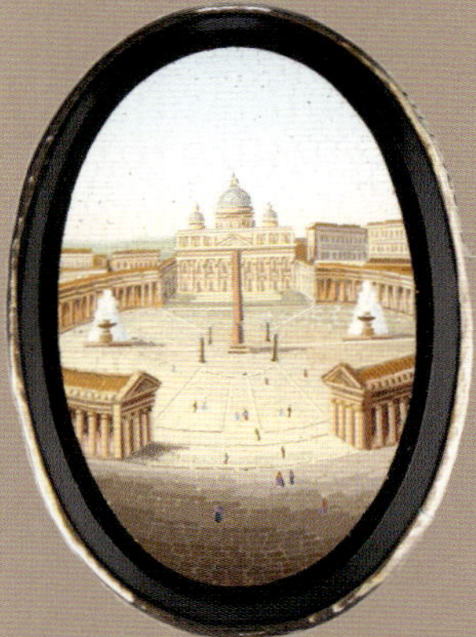

Left:
'Micro-mosaic' Brooch showing St Peter's Basilica, Italy, mid to late 19th century

Intricately-formed scenes made up of tiny tiles made from glass or other materials were popular items of jewellery during the Grand Tour period, and into the nineteenth century. The most common subjects included views of St Peter's – as here – and the Colosseum.

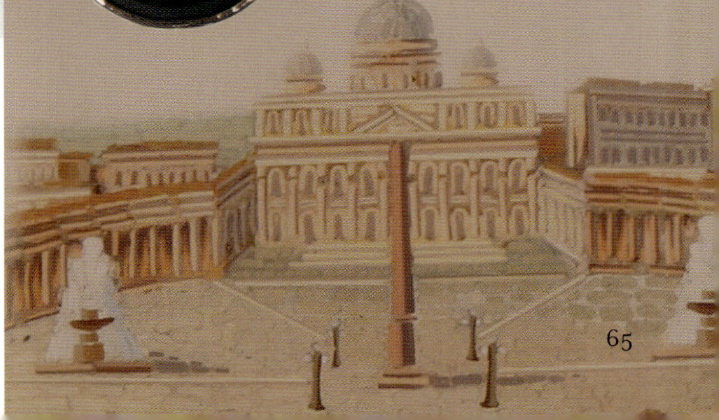

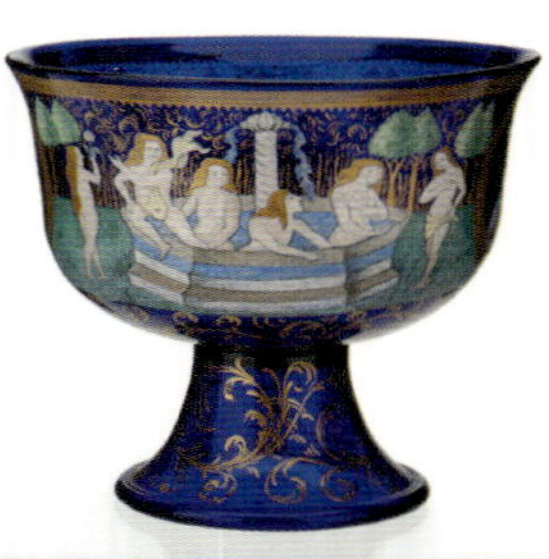

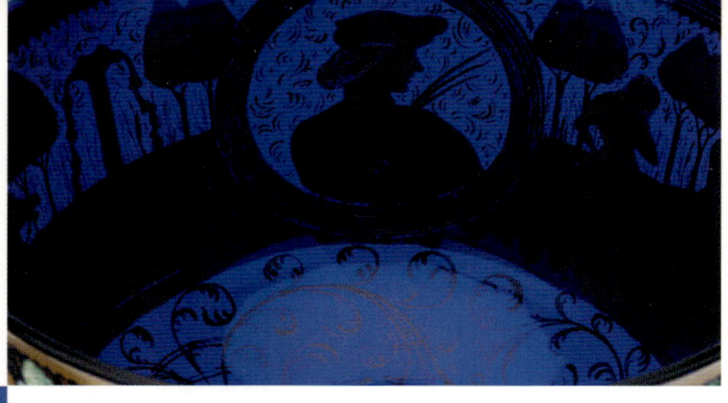

This bowl reproduces a Renaissance marriage goblet. Several original goblets survive, traditionally attributed to the Venetian glassmaker Angelo Barovier (who died in 1496). The goblets usually included portraits of the bride and groom and scenes of love and romance, including images of the 'fountain of youth', here to the right of the groom's portrait.

Cantagalli Factory and the Salviati Venetian Glass Companies

Ulisse Cantagalli and his brother revived the tradition of Renaissance-style maiolica making in Florence during the late 1870s. They were highly successful, and notably collaborated with the English master of lustreware William de Morgan. Their works are clearly marked with a cockerel, so could not be passed off as earlier pieces. Glasgow's finest Cantagalli ceramics were purchased in 1899, from an exhibition at the Victoria & Albert Museum.

Various companies made Renaissance and antique-style glass in Venice during the second half of the nineteenth century. Most were connected with Dr Antonio Salviati, who founded the Venice and Murano Glass Company in 1859. Between 1878 and 1899 over 30 fine pieces of this glass were purchased for Glasgow's collection. Many are stunningly ornate examples of the glassmakers' art, much showier than the earlier pieces. They were exhibited at international exhibitions, including that held in Paris in 1878.

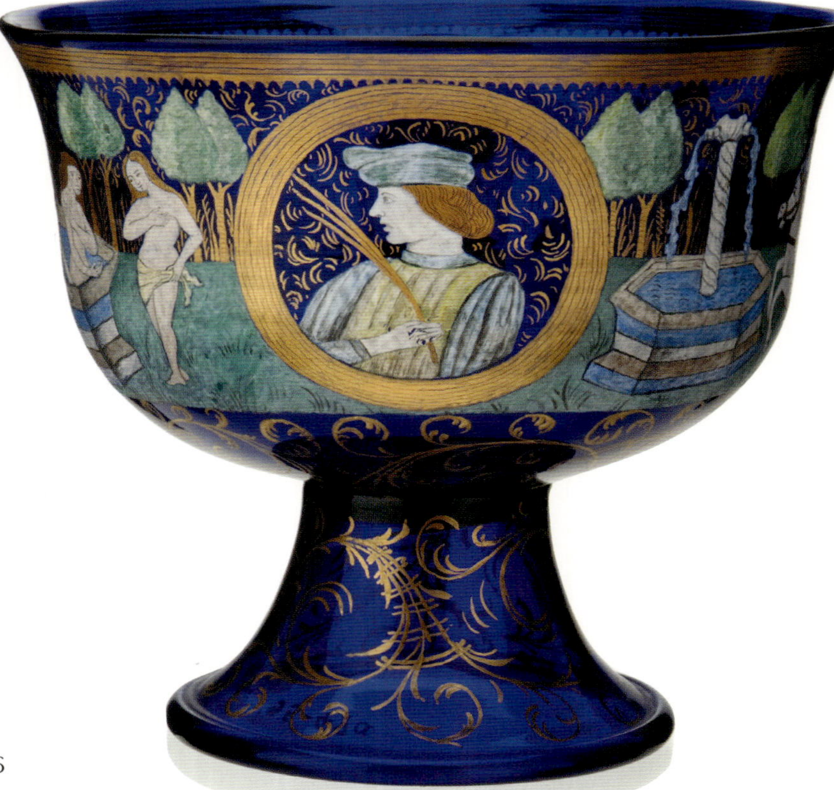

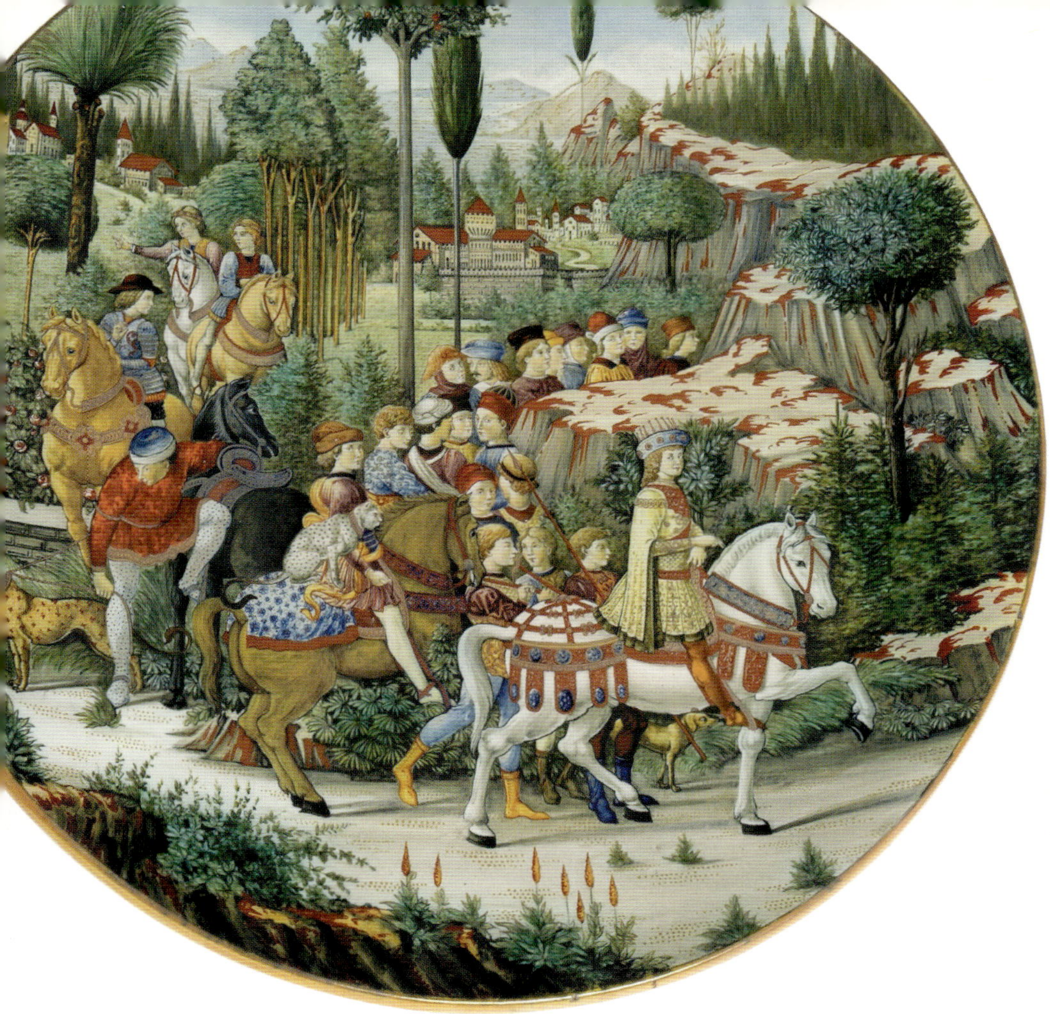

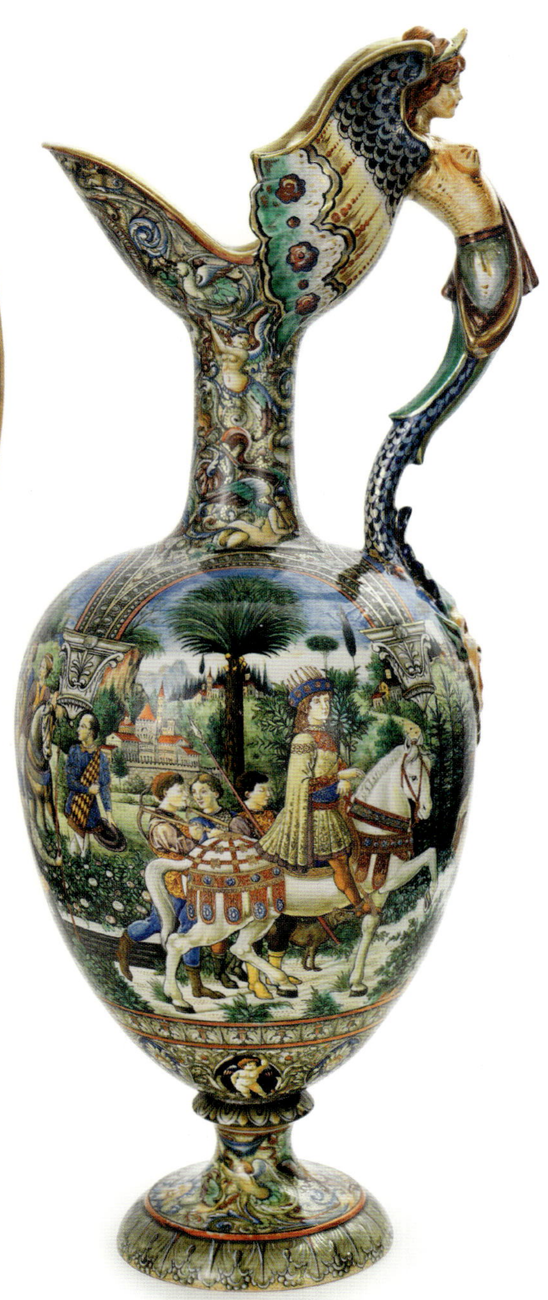

Dish and Ewer depicting the Journey of the Magi, *c.*1899
Florence, Cantagalli
Factory

These two Cantagalli pieces both depict a subject not found on Renaissance pottery. The scene of the *Journey of the Magi* is from a chapel painted in 1459–60 by Benozzo Gozzoli in the Medici Riccardi Palace in Florence. The transferral of this detailed scene to two differently-shaped ceramics was certainly a labour of love for the pottery-painters.

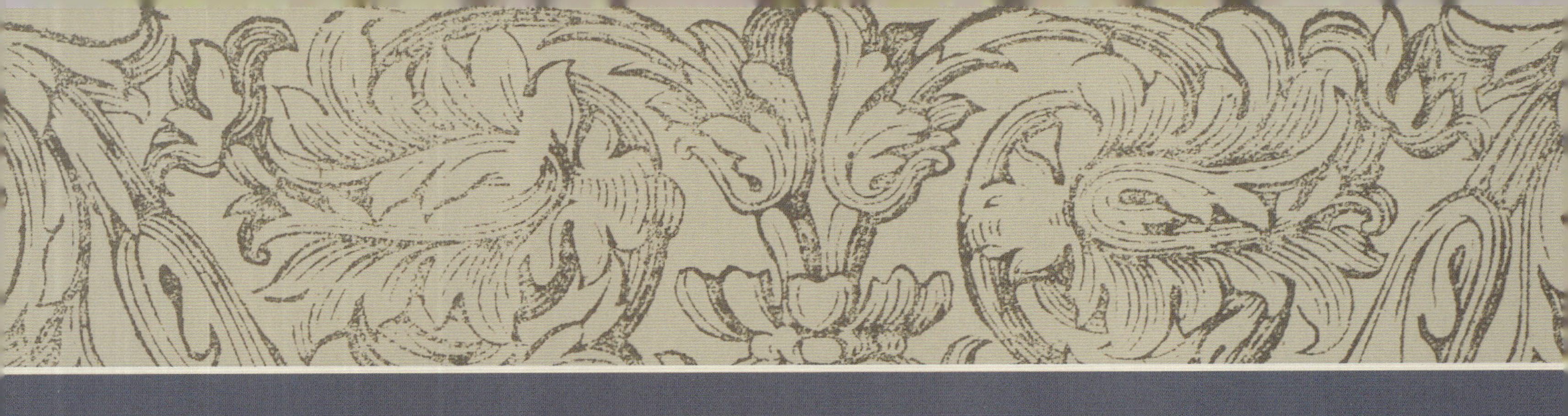

'*It would be no exaggeration to claim that Glasgow Museums house the finest and most comprehensive collection of Italian paintings of any civic museum in Britain.*'

Professor Peter Humfrey,
University of St Andrews

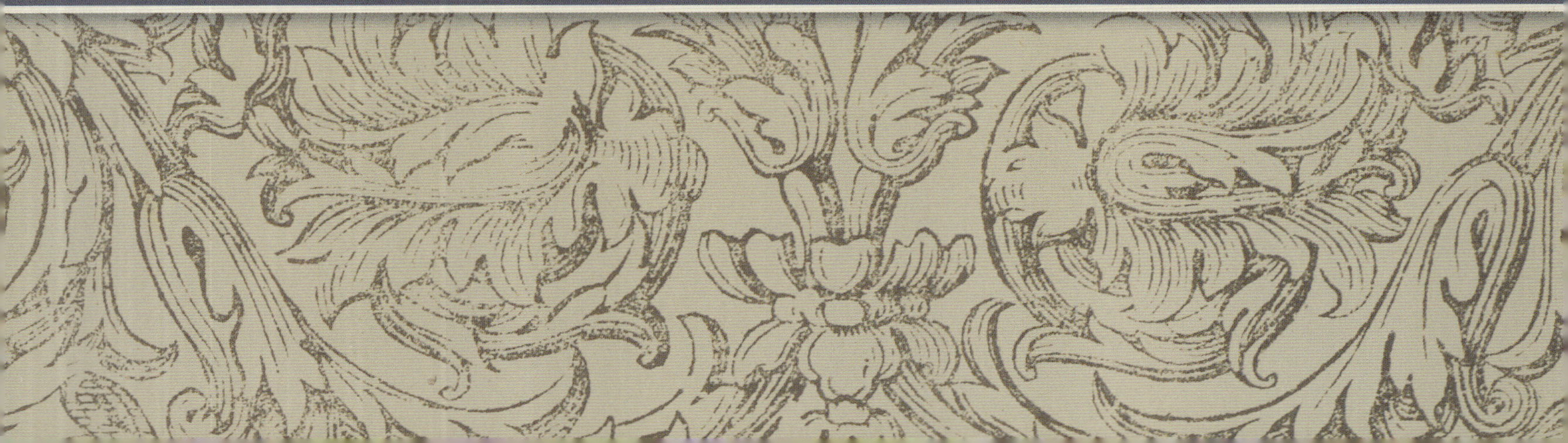